The

TWO KINGDOMS
STUDY GUIDE

DR. KEITH LANE

PREFACE

An individual's "death-experience" is related in this book. The death experience was shocking and traumatizing. Forever alienated and separated from God, living an eternal life of torment and agony.

Lack of understanding and complacency hinders some "Christian-Believers." Living a life that is an example to others requires focus, energy, and knowledge of JESUS.

I was a full-time College Instructor, in the Business Division of Fresno City College, for over thirty-seven (37) years. In some classes, I told a story about an "old-professor." He made a statement to his class: "Ignorance and apathy appear to be two major factors in our educational system." He then turned to a student and asked "what do you think of that?" The student responded: "I don't know and I don't care."

For some "Supposed-Christians," their life can be described as: Lack of "understanding" and "complacency."

This book is meant to identify issues that hinder Spiritual Maturity. There are only Two Kingdoms. The Kingdom of This World, and the Kingdom of God.

Individuals die daily without the "Saving-Knowledge" of Jesus Christ. I hope to be a catalyst for the "rebirth," "renewing," and "revival" of others.

This book is excellent for:
- Personal Growth
- Sunday School Classes
- Bible Study Groups
- Church-Home Study Groups

*For additional copies of this book contact:
kogtm@yahoo.com
www.kogtm.com
or

KINGDOM OF GOD TEACHING MINISTRIES
PO BOX 797
Kingsburg, CA 93631-0797

For speaking engagements contact:
keithlane39@yahoo.com
or

Dr. Keith Lane
KINGDOM OF GOD TEACHING MINISTRIES
PO BOX 797
Kingsburg, CA 93631-0797

*Additional discounts available for multiple copies.

ADDITIONAL FUNDS ARE USED FOR
GIFTING COPIES OF THIS BOOK TO:
SHELTER-MINISTRIES, MISSION-PROJECTS,
AND JAIL/PRISON-MINISTRIES.

DEDICATION

This book is dedicated to three (3) categories of individuals:

1. "Leaders" and those desiring to become Leaders.

Definition: I define a "leader" as an individual that is in a position to influence others. The influence is used to motivate others to: (a) "accept" Jesus Christ as Lord and Saviour, and (b) increase their "Spiritual Maturity."

2. "Believers" that cannot maintain a consistent "Christian-Life."

Definition: I define a "believer" as an individual that has "accepted" Jesus Christ as Lord and Saviour.

3. "Unbelievers" of Jesus Christ that do not understand why they need Him.

Definition: I define an "unbeliever" as a individual that has <u>not</u> "accepted" Jesus Christ as Lord and Saviour.

LEADERS:

I empathize with you because of the enormous "tasks" that God has called you to perform. Some of you have labored for many years and continue to labor. Many of you have little retirement and struggle financially. <u>Keep in mind, you are not home yet</u>. (Then, will God reveal those that have faithfully followed Him.) *Matthew 25:21: Well done, thou good and faithful servant: thou hast been faithful over a few things, I will make thee ruler over many things: enter thou into the joy of the Lord.*

May you continue to be motivated and assist other "<u>Souls</u>" (individuals) to enter into the "Kingdom of God." May God ignite a new desire, in your life, to see lives changed by Him. The harvest is white (ripe) unto harvest. This is a cooperative effort with others that have labored to "gather fruit unto life eternal." *John 4:35-38: 35. Say not ye, There are yet four months, and then cometh harvest? behold, I say unto you, Lift up your eyes, and look on the fields; for they are white already to harvest. 36. And he that reapeth receiveth wages, and gathereth fruit unto life eternal: that both he that soweth and he that reapeth may rejoice together. 37. And herein is that saying true, One soweth, and another reapeth. 38. I sent you to reap that whereon ye bestowed no labour: other men laboured, and ye are entered into their labours.*

BELIEVERS:

There is a "Spiritual-Battle" and you may get injured. Rise-up, again, in the name of Jesus and conquer all "enemies." The injuries you have received can cause you to empathize with others that have difficulties in their life. "Help," do not "hurt" others that are injured. The Christian Army seems to be the only Army that "kills" their wounded.

UNBELIEVERS:

Many individuals have never heard the message of Christ that makes "sense" to them. Their thinking may be: I'm not a bad person; I live a better life than most "supposed-Christians;" Why do I need Jesus Christ?

For you, I place in the beginning of this book why all people need Jesus Christ. See the next section entitled "Law of Propagation." Numerous sections of this book have been written for you. You may be an individual that was "raised" in church and have not come to "know" Jesus. The statement that you have been told "because the Bible says so," has not been sufficient for you. Hopefully, segments of this book will give you answers.

GET ON THE WINNING SIDE:

Work while you can! Jesus stated in John 9:4 there is coming a night when no man can work. *"I must work the works of him that sent me, while it is day: the night cometh, when no man can work."*

May we all be "worthy" to take part in the "Great-Harvest" that is about to occur.

LAW OF PROPAGATION

WHY YOU NEED JESUS CHRIST:

When Adam and Eve sinned (disobeyed), all of their future children would be born in their "likeness." By the Law of Propagation, each specie produces "after its own kind." Lions reproduce lions, corn reproduces corn, and "fallen-man" reproduces "fallen-man."

If you wanted to be smarter, you should have chosen smarter parents. Studies indicate the intelligence of a child is closely related to the average intelligence of the parents.

We have no choice of our genetic predisposition(s) and no choice of our "spiritual" inheritances. There are two (2) "blood-lines." First, the "blood-line" of Adam and secondly, the "blood-line" of Jesus Christ. Jesus' blood cleanses from all unrighteousness.

When, on the Cross of Calvary, Jesus said it is finished, it was done. Nothing else needs to be done. Only ask for "forgiveness" and take Jesus as Lord and Saviour.

TABLE OF CONTENTS:

SESSION ONE:

PLANNING AND GROUP FORMAT

First meeting is to meet and greet with individuals invited to join the Group. It is suggested during this meeting to read the recommendations written for the use of this Study Guide.

Those attending are encouraged to invite others to join for the next session, "Session Two."

RECOMMENDATIONS FOR USING THIS STUDY GUIDE:

SUGGESTED OUTLINE FORMAT FOR:
BIBLE STUDY GROUPS
and
CHURCH HOME GROUPS

1. Invite individuals to meet and possibly be a part of a Study Group.

2. Have copies available of the Book: TWO KINGDOMS and copies of this Study Guide. (These materials are designed to take thirteen (13) sessions.)

3. Determine how many individuals would like to Read the Book and use the Study Guide materials.

4. Determine the meeting time(s) and frequency of sessions, if not previously planned. (Are the sessions to be weekly, bi-weekly, or some other regular meeting time?)

5. Determine the length of the sessions. (The Study Guide Sessions are written to accommodate a time period of 45-60 minutes.)

6. Attempt to obtain a commitment from each individual in the Study Group to be prepared for each session.

7. EXAMPLE FOR A SESSION:

   a. Meet at 6:00 pm.

   b. Fellowship for 15-20 minutes. (Also allows flexibility for late-comers.)

   c. Begin meeting with a brief Prayer at 6:20 pm. (Establish and maintain, as closely as possible, the beginning scheduled times.) Without a consistent schedule, the meetings will not be as productive.

   d. Begin Study Time at 6:25 to 6:30 pm. (Again, establish and maintain, as closely as possible, the scheduled beginning times.)

   e. Enjoy the Study Time until 7:15 to 7:30 pm.

   f. If desired, another time of fellowship for 15-30 minutes after the Study time has ended.

BEGINNING STUDY GROUPS:

1. If the Bible Study Group or Church Home Study Group has a Facilitator:

   a. Include as many people as possible.

   b. When reading the assigned segments from the book, either read the entire materials yourself or ask for volunteers to read. Never rotate around the group or call on an unsuspecting individual. (Some individuals do not like to read in public. These individuals may not mention this fact, but they will stop attending.)

   c. It is suggested you gently remind your group of social protocol(s). The protocols should be restated for the first few sessions and as often as you deem necessary.

SUGGESTIONS TO PARTICIPANTS:

   (1) Give others an opportunity to participate.

   (2) Please limit your comments. (Do not monopolize the

Group's Time.) It is suggested verbal comments should not exceed three (3) minutes, per question, by any group-member.

(3) There should be a "friendly reminder" if some individuals continue "on-and-on."

(4) The establishment and mentioning of the "Suggestions to Participants" will inhibit potential "group frustration."

d. At the opening of your first few sessions:

(1) Develop and maintain a format for the exchange of communication and feedback. (A brief mentioning of the "Suggestions to Participants.")

(2) Restate the length of verbal comments by individuals.

(3) Restate the time and place of the sessions.

(4) Restate the length of the sessions.

(5) Solicit a contact-person that maintains the names, addresses, telephone numbers and other personal "contact-information."

(6) Most groups have better attendance by a reminder (call or e-mail) within seventy-two (72) hours of the scheduled meeting.

(7) Allowing newcomers to join the study group. (Best results are obtained by a flexible attitude.) In other words, do not exclude individuals if they want to join. Individuals are able to "catch-up" by personally studying the sections they have missed.

2. If the Study Group or Church Home Group does NOT have a Facilitator:

a. A good Leader or Facilitator is vital to the group.

b. If possible, a Facilitator that has a "history" of good teaching would be an excellent choice.

All other comments under "SUGGESTIONS TO PARTICIPANTS" (Page 13) should be followed, as a guide, after selecting a Facilitator.

3. If the Study Group is a Sunday School Class:

    a. The materials of this book are ideal for Sunday School Classes.

    b. If you are the teacher of a class and are obtaining good results, then continue with your present "teaching style."

    c. If you are beginning a new section or series using this book, then encourage members to bring friends with them.

    d. If there are individuals, in an existing class, that monopolize class time, attempt to tactfully incorporate the applicable "SUGGESTIONS TO PARTICIPANTS" (Page 13).

FAITH

For many years, I have lived in the San Joaquin Valley of Central California, one of the largest and most productive farm areas in the world. To produce a crop of tomatoes, beans or cantaloupes, it requires three (3) items. (In addition, I will correlate these items to the development and growth of faith.) These three (3) items are:

1. Seed
2. Water
3. Sunshine

SEED:

The seed must be planted in fertile soil. Water is needed to moisten the seed and soil. Sunshine is needed to warm the seed, soil, and plant. Sunshine is required for the process of photosynthesis. Photosynthesis is the process when a plant absorbs light (sunshine) and cellular growth occurs.

Each individual has been given a measure of faith. However, unless this seed of faith is in fertile soil, it will not propagate (grow and reproduce). The seed of faith remains dormant in many individuals their entire life.

WATER:

The watering of the seed and soil, with sufficient sunshine develops the seed. The watering of the seed of faith is accomplished by the "hearing" of

God's Word. "Hearing" the Word of God is not just listening, reading and studying God's Word. "Hearing" of God's Word is related to "obedience." Obeying (acting upon) a command or instruction indicates an individual heard the command. Faith comes by hearing and hearing by the word of God. Some individuals have never heard the Word of God. Some individuals believe they have heard the Word of God, but actually have not heard the Word because they do not "obey." In fact, the Bible, in James 1:22 states: "But be ye doers of the word, and not hearers only, deceiving your own selves." The washing (cleansing) by the Word of God.

Ephesians: 5:26-27:

26. That he might sanctify and cleanse it (the church) with the washing of water by the word, 27. That he might present it to himself a glorious church, not having spot, or wrinkle, or any such thing; but that it should be holy and without blemish.

SUNSHINE:

Sunshine (light) relates to the Love of God. (God is Light and God is Love) The maturation of a plant (individual) is directly proportional to the amount of light it receives. A plant needs good soil and light to produce a mature and abundant harvest.

Loving God and loving others is the fulfillment of the law.

Luke 10:25-27:

25. And, behold, a certain lawyer stood up, and tempted him, saying, Master, what shall I do to inherit eternal life? 26. He said unto him, What is written in the law? How readest thou? 27. And he answering said, Thou shalt love the Lord thy God with all thy heart, and with all thy soul, and with all thy strength, and with all thy mind; and thy neighbour as thyself.

Hopefully, as you use this Study Guide, your faith and Spiritual maturity will increase. Teaching (instruction) is the anecdotal remedy for lack of faith. Individuals need to know and follow correct horticultural methods to grow good crops. Faith comes by hearing and hearing by the word of God. (Romans 10:17) Individuals need to know and obey the steps related to developing additional faith. Notice the sequence of steps Paul delineates in Romans 10:14-21.

Romans 10:14-21:

14. ...how shall they hear without a preacher?

16. An individual may have heard, but they have not obeyed.

18. They have heard, but they have not heard.

20. God states Israel is a disobedient people.

FAITH GROWS:

Luke 17:6:

6. And the Lord said, If ye had faith as a grain of mustard seed, ye might say unto this sycamine tree, Be thou plucked up by the root, and be thou planted in the sea; and it should obey you.

Mark 11:23:

For verily I say unto you, That whosoever shall say unto this mountain, Be thou removed, and be thou cast into the sea; and shall not doubt in his heart, but shall believe that those things which he saith shall come to pass; he shall have whatsoever he saith.

Every individual is given a measure of faith. Romans 12:3 states: "For I say, through the grace given unto me, to every man that is among you, not to think of himself more highly than he ought to think; but to think soberly, according as God hath dealt to every man the measure of faith."

The measure of faith given to each individual will remain small unless it is developed. The rapidity of growth is directly proportional to the following:

1. Hearing (Hear the word of God)

2. Obeying (Obey the word of God)

3. Loving (Love God and Others)

MUSTARD SEED FAITH:

The initial measure of faith will remain small without the proper growth environment. With the proper nutrients and environment, the mustard seed will grow into a tree. In fact, Jesus states the greatest among herbs. Even birds can lodge in the branches.

Matthew 13:31-32:

31. Another parable put he forth unto them, saying, The kingdom of heaven is like to a grain of mustard seed, which a man took, and sowed in his field: 32. Which indeed is the least of all seeds: but when it is grown, it is the greatest among herbs, and becometh a tree, so that the birds of the air come and lodge in the branches thereof.

MOUNTAIN MOVING FAITH:

If faith grows to a level of high maturity, it can even move mountains. However, love is more important than faith. Paul writes in I Corinthians 13:2: "And though I have the gift of prophecy, and understand all mysteries, and all knowledge; and though I have all faith, so that I could remove mountains, and have not charity, I am nothing."

**LOVE IS MORE
IMPORTANT THAN FAITH!**

A mountain will not be moved with mustard seed faith. Just as a mustard seed develops and grows, faith should develop and grow. There are other examples, in the Bible, of "growing-faith." Immediately after Jesus spoke of the mustard seed, He gave the example of the growth of the kingdom of heaven.

Matthew 13:33:

Another parable spake he unto them; The kingdom of heaven is like unto leaven, which a woman took, and hid in three measures of meal, till the whole was leavened.

UNDEVELOPED FAITH:

Jesus teaches why his disciples could not cast out a certain type of demonic spirit.

The disciples had attempted to cure the lunatic son but had failed. The father, of the lunatic son, brought the son to Jesus and told Him (Jesus) of the failure by His disciples. Jesus rebuked the devil and the child was immediately cured. Then, the disciples wanted to know why they did not have a successful curing of the child. Jesus gives them a teaching on faith. Jesus' answer to His disciples referred to their unbelief indicating an undeveloped or small amount of faith. You failed because of your unbelief and He (Jesus) again relates the story (example) of mustard seed faith and mountain moving faith. In addition, he teaches there are hierarchies of demonic powers. Your faith has worked in the other situations you have encountered, but with this type prayer and fasting is required.

Matthew 17:15-21:

15. Lord, have mercy on my son: for he is lunatick, and sore vexed: for ofttimes he falleth into the fire, and oft into the water. 16. And I brought him to thy disciples, and they could not cure him. 17. Then Jesus answered and said, O faithless and perverse generation, how long shall I be with you? How long shall I suffer you? Bring him hither to me. 18. And Jesus rebuked the devil; and he departed out of him: and the child was cured from that very hour. 19. Then came the disciples to Jesus apart, and said, Why could not we cast him out? 20. And Jesus said unto them, Because of your unbelief: for verily I say unto you, If ye have faith as a grain of mustard seed, ye shall say unto this mountain, Remove hence to yonder place; and it shall remove; and nothing shall be impossible unto you. 21. Howbeit this kind goeth not out but by prayer and fasting.

WORKING FAITH:

Each individual has received a measure of faith. However, there are various stages (degrees) of growth in developing faith. I will give two examples to indicate the "growth concept" of faith.

Example One: (A Physics Principle)

If a transport (movement) of weight is needed, force is required to move the weight. The Principle of Physics is the greater the weight to be moved, the greater the force (energy) required. A car cannot move a trainload of weight. In fact, even a single locomotive engine cannot exert sufficient force to move (pull) weights in mountainous terrain. I have seen as many as six (6) locomotive engines being used in mountainous terrain.

Example Two: (A Monetary Concept)

Let us set a monetary value to the initial measure of faith given to each individual as a penny (1-cent). Different levels of faith are required to resolve individual problems. If a "five-dollar" problem is encountered, the initial measure of faith does not resolve the problem. In the Spirit, there are problems beyond the "five-dollar" problem. There may be "fifty-dollar" problems and greater.

DEVELOPING FAITH:

Do not attempt to move beyond your measure of developed faith. I have observed numerous individuals become overwhelmed, frustrated and eventually just give-up their Christian experience. This "giving-up" is a result of improper (false) teaching related to faith. Only individuals of humility, using faith that glorifies God and brings health and healing to His Body is "proper" faith. In fact, any act or display of faith that draws excessive attention to an individual is a misuse of faith. Individuals fail because of their lack of understanding and misuse of faith. Incorrect (false) teaching regarding faith initiates personal exercises in presumptuous faith.

One individual, an acquaintance, had a job as a fireman. He became engulfed in a false perception concerning faith. He began to proclaim, on his job, there would be no fires in the city while he was on duty. Of course, there were fires and he became frustrated. He quit his good job and went to a "faith-school" in the mid-western United States. His family deteriorated and ultimately he was divorced and now is attempting to financially survive.

Another individual placed a picture of an airplane on his refrigerator and proclaimed that he was receiving the plane by faith. He was very adamant that he was going to get the airplane. Any questioning or external controversy he labeled as negative and would not listen to reason. This individual is now deceased. He failed at his business, never received his airplane and remained frustrated because of guilt-feelings for not being able to understand why his dreams were not realized.

Another individual, a friend and associate pastor of a church, became "fixed" upon his ability to move God's hand. He was ensnared by grandeur visions of church growth. He became frustrated, quit the ministry and divorced his lovely wife. All three (3) of these individuals were associated in the same church. Additionally, two (2) others associated with them were overwhelmed by the same false teacher. This "supposed" man of faith has initiated a travesty of devastation to many individuals and their families. The proclamation of false teachings by immature leaders is dangerous and has caused devastation to numerous individuals desiring to enter further into the Kingdom of God.

The Two Kingdoms Study Guide

AREAS IN LIVES THAT
NEED CLEANSING:

Numerous topics in this Study Guide indicate areas that need "cleansing" in our personal temple. The areas mentioned in this Study Guide that need "cleansing" include:

1. LACK OF FORGIVENESS – (SESSION FIVE)

2. COMPLAINING – (SESSIONS SIX, SEVEN, EIGHT and NINE)

3. IDOLATRY – (SESSION ELEVEN)

4. PORNOGRAPHY – (SESSION TWELVE)

SESSION TWO:

TWO KINGDOMS

Read Pages: 13-25 of the book entitled "Two Kingdoms."

There are two Kingdoms defined in the Bible. The first is the "Kingdom of This World," and the second is the "Kingdom of God."

KINGDOM OF THIS WORLD:

The Kingdom of This World is also known as the "Kingdom of Darkness." The father and leader of this Kingdom is the Devil. Individuals that are members of this Kingdom manifest "works of the flesh." The "works of the flesh," manifest specific behaviors and actions. These behaviors and actions are what the Bible refers to as "works of the flesh." These individuals will not inherit or become a part of the "Kingdom of God."

Galatians 5:19-21:

19. Now the works of the flesh are manifest, which are these; Adultery, fornication, uncleanness, lasciviousness, 20. Idolatry, witchcraft, hatred, variance, emulations, wrath, strife, seditions, heresies, 21. Envyings, murders, drunkenness, revellings, and such like: of the which I tell you before, as I have also told you in time past, that they which do such things shall not inherit the Kingdom of God.

There is a natural body, and there is a spiritual body. *I Corinthians 15:44: It is sown a natural body; it is raised a spiritual body, There is a natural body, and there is a spiritual body.* All individuals have a natural body and receive a "soul-life."

The natural (earthly) man does not receive the things of God. In fact, they are foolish to him. *I Corinthians 2:14: But the natural man receiveth not the things of the Spirit of God: for they are foolishness unto him: neither can he know them, because they are spiritually discerned.*

Those of this Kingdom, the "Kingdom of This World," are in darkness and are blinded to the gravity and seriousness of their situation. Individuals of this Kingdom are alienated from God. At birth, all individuals are born into this Kingdom. You have to do nothing to retain membership in the "Kingdom of This World." The Father of the Kingdom of This World is the Devil. He will encourage you to "be yourself." Enjoy this life and the lustful behaviors and actions you want to do. "You only live once." This Kingdom is a Kingdom of "Self-Centered" and "Selfish" individuals.

QUESTION:

1. Why are the behaviors listed in Galations 5:19-21 referred to as "works of the flesh?"

_____

_____

_____

_____

2. Why do all individuals have these common behaviors (works of the flesh)?

_____

_____

_____

_____

_____

3. Why must all individuals receive Jesus Christ as Lord and Savior?

_____

_____

_____

_____

4. Why do some individuals of the "Kingdom of This World" or the "Kingdom of Darkness," supposedly, live a better moral life than some individuals professing Christianity? Briefly explain.

_____

_____

_____

_____

LOVERS OF SELF:

Narcissism means "Self-Love" or "Lover of Self." Self-Love is a prominent attribute for those in the "Kingdom of This World." Paul, when writing to Timothy, instructs and describes these individuals.

II Timothy 3:1-7:

1. This know also, that in the last days perilous times shall come. 2. For men shall be lovers of their own selves, covetous, boasters, proud, blasphemers, disobedient to parents, unthankful, unholy, 3. Without natural affection, trucebreakers, false accusers, incontinent, fierce, despisers of those that are good. 4. Traitors, heady, highminded, lovers of pleasures more than lovers of God. 5. Having a form of godliness, but denying the power thereof: from such turn away. 6. For of this sort are they which creep into houses, and lead captive silly women laden with sins, led away with divers lusts, 7. Ever learning, and never able to come to the knowledge of the truth.

Paul, in the book of Romans, gives further details relating the traits and attributes of individuals in the "Kingdom of Darkness." As you read the information in this Chapter, if you discover any of the traits or attributes in your life, you are not a part of the "Kingdom of God." In Romans 1:24, God gives these individuals "up" to uncleanness. In Romans 1:26, God gives these individuals "up" to vile affections. In Romans 1:28, God gives these individuals "over" to a "reprobate-mind." A "reprobate-mind" is a "mind" void of the ability to make logical decisions. Notice the downward progression as individuals become more polluted and perverted. God gives them "up," "up," and finally "over." Because of the clear message contained in the First Chapter of Romans, I want to print the entire chapter.

Romans Chapter One:

1. Paul, a servant of Jesus Christ, called to be an apostle, separated unto the gospel of God, 2. (Which he had promised afore by his prophets in the holy scriptures,) 3. Concerning his Son Jesus Christ our Lord, which was made of the seed of David according to the flesh; 4. And declared to be the Son of God with power, according to the spirit of holiness, by the resurrection from the dead: 5. By whom we have received grace and apostleship, for obedience to the faith among all nations, for his name: 6. Among whom are ye also the called of Jesus Christ: 7. To all that be in Rome, beloved of God, called to be saints: Grace to you and peace from our Father, and the Lord Jesus Christ. 8. First, I thank my God through Jesus Christ for you all, that your faith is spoken of throughout the whole world. 9. For God is my witness, whom I serve with my spirit in the gospel of his Son, that without ceasing I make mention of you always in my prayers; 10. Making request, if by any means now at length I might have a prosperous journey by the will of God to come unto you. 11. For I long to see you, that I may impart unto you some spiritual gift, to the end ye may be established; 12. That is, that I may be comforted together with you by the mutual faith both of you and me. 13. Now I would not have you ignorant, brethren, that oftentimes I purposed to come unto you, (but was let hitherto,) that I might have some fruit among you also, even as among other Gentiles. 14. I am debtor both to the Greeks, and to the Barbarians; both to the wise, and to the unwise. 15. So, as much as in me is, I am ready to preach the gospel to you that are at Rome also. 16. For I am not ashamed of the gospel of Christ: for it is the power of God unto salvation to every one that believeth; to the Jew first, and also to the Greek. 17. For therein is the righteousness of God revealed from faith to faith: as it is written, The just shall live by faith. 18. For the wrath of God is revealed from heaven against all ungodliness and unrighteousness of men, who hold the truth in unrighteousness; 19. Because that which may be known of God is manifest in them; for God hath shewed it unto them. 20. For the invisible things of him from the creation of the world are clearly seen, being understood by the things that are made, even his eternal power and Godhead; so that they are without excuse: 21. Because that, when they knew God, they glorified him not as God, neither were thankful; but became vain in their imaginations, and their foolish heart was darkened. 22. Professing themselves to be wise, they became fools, 23.And changed the glory of the uncorruptible God into an image made like to corruptible man, and to birds, and four-footed beasts, and creeping things. 24. Wherefore God also gave them up to uncleanness through the lusts of their own hearts, to dishonour their own bodies between themselves: 25. Who changed the truth of God into a lie, and worshipped and served the creature more than the Creator, who is blessed for ever. Amen. 26. For this cause God gave them up unto vile affections: for even their women did change the natural use into that which is against nature: 27. And likewise also the men, leaving the natural use of the woman, burned in their lust one toward another; men with men working that which is unseemly, and receiving in themselves that recompence of their error which was meet. 28. And even as they did not like to retain God in their knowledge, God gave them over to a reprobate mind, to do those things which are not convenient; 29. Being filled with all unrighteousness, fornication, wickedness, covetousness, maliciousness; full of envy, murder, debate, deceit, malignity; whisperers, 30. Backbiters, haters of God, despiteful, proud, boasters, inventors of evil things, disobedient to parents, 31. Without understanding, covenantbreakers, without natural affection, implacable, unmerciful: 32. Who knowing the judgment of God, that they which commit such things are worthy of death, not only do the same, but have pleasure in them that do them.

Remaining a member of this "Kingdom of Darkness" will lead an individual to eternal separation from God. Unless an individual is "Born of God," they will experience "Eternal Death." "Eternal Death" is also known as the "Second Death." The "Second Death" is explained later in this book. (See page 56 for the topic entitled: Explanation of "Eternal Death.")

QUESTION:

5. Narcissism is "Love of Self." How do we notice Narcissism in our:

    a. Personal and Spiritual Life?

_____

_____

_____

_____

_____

    b. Home-life (Immediate family and extended family members)?

_____
_____
_____
_____
_____

c. Friends and Church Community?

_____
_____
_____
_____
_____

d. Work Relationships?

_____
_____
_____
_____
_____

e. Have you identified areas, in your life, that need changes? Yes___
No___
If yes, take **PERSONAL NOTES**:

_____
_____
_____
_____
_____

KINGDOM OF GOD:

This Kingdom is a "Kingdom of Light." The Father of this Kingdom is God. The leader of this Kingdom is Jesus Christ, God's Only Begotten Son. Individuals that are members of this Kingdom manifest certain behaviors and actions. These behaviors and actions are referred to, in the Bible, as "Fruits of the Spirit." The members of this Kingdom have "crucified" (made null or dead) the "works of the flesh."

Galatians 5:22-24:

22. But the fruit of the Spirit is love, joy, peace, longsuffering, gentleness, goodness, faith, 23. Meekness, temperance: against such there is no law. 24. And they that are Christ's have crucified the flesh with the affections and lusts.

QUESTION:

6. Do you believe it is possible to speed-up your Spiritual Growth?
Yes___ No___

What are the reason(s) you believe your response is correct?

_____

_____

_____

_____

_____

OB PORTU:

Portions of this section were researched and quoted from the following web site: http://www.actsweb.org/articles

Prior to modern harbors, a ship had to wait for the flood tide to make it into port. The ports were not developed and ships suffered loss, especially sailing ships, if the timing for portal entry was incorrect. The phrase for this "timing," in Latin, was called ob portu. The word "opportunity" is derived from this Latin phrase. Opportunity comes to <u>pass</u>, not to <u>pause</u>. A ship's captain wanting to enter port had to wait for the moment when the tide was exactly right to carry the ship to harbor.

The captain and the crew waited for the precise moment when the tide was right, because they knew if they missed it; they would have to wait for another tidal entry.

NOW IS THE TIME OF SALVATION, THIS OPPORTUNITY MAY NOT COME AGAIN DURING YOUR LIFETIME. Now is the time to make things right with God. IF YOU WANT TO MAKE IT TO THE "PORTALS OF HEAVEN," NOW IS THE TIME!

QUESTION:

7. If you have asked Jesus to forgive you of your sins and have accepted Him (Jesus) as your Personal Savior, answer the following:

   a. Are you presently as excited about being a Christian as you were when you first became a Christian? Yes___ No___ Explain your response.

   _____
   _____
   _____
   _____
   _____

   b. What are some of the reasons individuals lose their Spiritual Motivation? Briefly explain.

c. What can individuals do to maintain consistency in their "Christian-Walk?" Briefly explain.

d. How could the Church do a better job ministering to the needs of others? Briefly explain.

e. What can individuals do to assist those within their sphere of influence? Briefly explain.

DAVE'S GOT RELIGION:

Dave's mother and older sister were members of the small church I attended. During a revival, when I was a teenager, Dave came to church. He went to the altar and repented of his sins. Dave was approximately twenty-three (23) years of age. As Dave was leaving the church, his "drinking-buddies" drove by, laughed and shouted loudly: "Dave's Got Religion!"

To my knowledge, Dave never attended church again. When he was in his sixties (60's); while angry, he went outside, placed a gun to his head and committed suicide. What a shame, Dave did not have the courage to stand against a public ridicule.

Dave missed an opportunity to enter
the "portals of heaven,"
don't miss yours!

Dave's father never attended church. His mother and sister were dedicated to "serving" God, but the boys were allowed to stay home rather than attend church.

A Christian foundation is important. I was held in my Grandfather's arms and dedicated at the age of four (4). My older cousins were playing "hide-and-seek." I was telling where everyone was hid and they wanted to get rid of me. A rabbit or fox ran into a wood pile area. They told me they were mean and would bite the smallest person around and that I should run to Grandpa.

My grandfather was a lay-Methodist Minister. He spent hours studying the Bible and Praying. He also had a blacksmith shop on his small farm. This day, he was in his small barn area praying. I remember the occasion well. He was dressed in his overalls; kneeling in prayer, and crying. Grandpa was safety to me. If I needed help, I ran to grandpa.

I came to him, while he was kneeling in prayer, and snuggled right into him. After a few moments he picked me up, while still on his knees, held me in front of him and dedicated me. I can still remember most of his prayer. His prayer was that God would be with me all of my life; that I would have a long and prosperous life; and the same Spirit that dwelled in him would dwell in me.

From that day of dedication, I have had a hunger for God. I have always loved God. I have always enjoyed reading, especially the Bible. Most adult-years of my life, I have read the Bible through (from the beginning of Genesis to the end of Revelation). Some years of my life, I have read the Bible completely through two (2) or three (3) times.

At age sixteen (16), I was very involved as youth leader in my church. I spent hours each day memorizing and reading scripture. I enjoyed school and carried my 3x5 cards with memory verses to learn new scripture and retain previously memorized scripture.

All of my grandfather's prayers for me have "come-to-pass." I married into a wonderful family and after fifty (50) years of marriage, God continues to bless us. My wife also came to Jesus at a very young age. Her older sister says she got Louise "saved" during a revival at the age of three (3). What a great life. Every child, grandchild, my siblings and their spouses, my wife's siblings and their spouses and children, all "serve the Lord." Our immediate family, a daughter and son, are both very successful. Daughter is an attorney and my son is back in school obtaining another degree (Master's Degree in Business Administration). Our family has received both financial and Spiritual Blessings. Our daughter-in-law has completed her Master's Degree in Administration, presently a High School English Teacher. One granddaughter is a Nurse, and is completing her Master's Degree in Nursing. One grand-son-in-law has completed his Master's Degree in Math and teaching in a High School and College. HOWEVER, THEIR GREATEST ACCOMPLISHMENT IS "THEY ALL SERVE THE LORD."

Dave did not have a foundation. His father was not a good example for him. No image of "greatness" or "stature" was birthed into him. There was no concept of what God wanted to do in his life.

What a shame that a little ridicule isolates and discourages some individuals. YOU BE A PERSON OF "STATURE." Attempt, with all that is in you, to be an example of what God can do in a life.

QUESTION:

8. What causes individuals to be so influenced by the opinions of others? Briefly explain.

_____

_____

_____

_____

9. What can individuals do to maintain a strong "Christian-Walk" and ignore the opinions of others? Briefly explain.

_____

_____

_____

_____

10. What, if anything, can an individual do to change their "mind-set?" "Mind-set" is defined as an individual's usual (normal) thinking pattern(s). Briefly explain.

_____

_____

_____

_____

_____

ETERNAL IMPORTANCE:

This is an extremely important personal decision. If you are not for certain, that you have accepted JESUS CHRIST into your life; now is the time to accept Him. STOP WHAT YOU ARE DOING AND GET PRIVACY IF YOU CAN. Speak these words, audibly (out loud) in "Faith" believing:

SALVATION PRAYER
JESUS, I ask your forgiveness of all my sins.
I am sorry for all the hurts I have caused,
to myself and to others.
I truly want you to change my life.
I want to give myself completely to you.
May I know the Peace and Joy
that only you can give.
I want to be an example to
those around me of
how you can change a life.

QUESTION:

11. Do you have recommendations for the Salvation Prayer? Yes___ No___ If so, please indicate those recommendations or, if you prefer, write another simple Salvation Prayer.

_____

_____

_____

_____

_____

_____

_____

_____

_____

If you prayed this Prayer, Congratulations! You have taken the first step in becoming what God intended you to be during this earthly life.

In addition, if you are "non-committed" in your "Christian-Life," you need to become determined and focused upon Jesus. Allowing Jesus to live His life through you is the "Christian-Life." Do not confuse living a "good-life" and "giving" your life to Jesus.

Individuals with "good-intentions" are not automatically members of the Kingdom of God. Repent of <u>all</u> your sins and allow Jesus complete access to your life.

If you have <u>not</u> been living a "clean" and "pure" life, you need to make changes in your life. <u>Now</u> is the time to change. STOP WHAT YOU ARE DOING AND GET PRIVACY IF YOU CAN. Speak these words, audibly (out loud) in "Faith" believing:

REDEDICATION PRAYER

<u>**Renewed Commitment**</u>
JESUS, I ask your forgiveness of all my sins,
I want to rededicate my life to you.
I am sorry for all the hurts I have caused,
to myself and to others.
I truly want you to change my life.
I want to give myself completely to you.
May I know the Peace and Joy
that only you can give.
I want to be an example to
those around me of
how you can change a life.
I rededicate my life and will serve
you with all of my heart.

"Good-intentions" do not guarantee a continued "placement" in the Kingdom of God. Determine to remain "focused" and "committed" for the rest of your life.

If you prayed the prayer of forgiveness or the prayer of "renewed commitment," I would like to hear from you. If you received Jesus into your life or were encouraged by this book, please let me know at the following address:

Dr. Keith Lane
KINGDOM OF GOD TEACHING MINISTRIES
PO BOX 797
Kingsburg, CA 93631-0797
keithlane39@yahoo.com

MY PERSONAL PRAYER TO ALL WHO RECEIVE AND READ THIS BOOK IS: YOU ALLOW GOD CONTINUED ENTRANCE IN YOUR LIFE AND THAT HE WILL BLESS YOU AND KEEP YOU IN HIS CARE.

RECEIVE HIS GRACE AND FORGIVENESS.

QUESTION:

12. Do you have recommendations for the Rededication Prayer?
    Yes___ No___ If so, please indicate those recommendations or, if you prefer, write another simple Rededication Prayer.

_____
_____
_____
_____
_____
_____
_____
_____
_____

**REMAIN A MEMBER OF
THE KINGDOM OF GOD!**

SESSION THREE:

UNIQUE EXPERIENCE

Read Pages: 26-35 of the book entitled "Two Kingdoms."

A deposit of God is within each of us. John 1:9 declares that Jesus was the true Light, which lighteth every man that cometh into the world.

During a flight in September of 2010, I sat next to a young professional lady. After a brief exchange she stated to me "I don't normally share this, but I had a death experience that changed my life and I will share it with you."

She briefly shared that during her "death period," she encountered two distinct experiences. One a very positive experience and another experience that was extremely negative. She stated that during her "death period," she was aware of her entire life. The experience was a panoramic view of her earthly existence. She sensed that God was showing her two options.

Her first experience (option) was that God is conscious of each individual and there is the possibility of an eternal experience of Love, Comfort, and a connectedness to God. She believed this Love and Comfort is magnified exponentially to what most "Christians" comprehend and understand. This was an experience of bright and beautiful light. There was no awareness of "time." She only experienced great Joy, exuberant Delight, immense Peace and a sense of ecstatic Satisfaction.

Her second experience (option) was a horrible existence. She stated: "It seemed as though all the negative emotional feelings that I ever experienced were simultaneously being experienced." During this experience, there was total darkness, a complete absence of light. Although she could not see them, she was aware that there were demonic forces all around her. This experience was "time-related." Each moment, however brief, seemed never to pass. In addition, there was an overwhelming consciousness that there would never be an escape. She would be in this situation eternally.

She stated these two experiences had changed her thinking and her life. During this brief period, she sensed a personal awareness from God. Many "Christians" concern themselves with sins, but the sins that are of greater significance are those sins that cause hurt and impact negatively other individuals. She said that she was aware of hurts she had caused during her life and had no idea of the immense anguish and pain she had caused other individuals. Therefore, at this time, she stated, "I am much more aware and cautious of how I treat others."

She continued and stated, "You may think this is odd and laugh, but God imparted three personal messages to me. First, I will have a significant Grandmother's role. I have children, but I still do not know if the children will be from my children or the children of other individuals. However, I am supposed to have a Grandmother's role. Secondly, I will not be a public speaker, but I will share my experience in 'one-to-one' relationships." Thirdly, she continued, "I sensed I had no responsibility to share my experience in a public manner." Then, a succinct statement to me, "possibly, you will be a person that will share my experience with others."

At that time, she could not have been aware that I was in the process of writing this book and specifically finishing the segment regarding "Eternal Death." This brief encounter encouraged me to delineate in greater detail the auspices and gravity of "Separation from God" and the "Second Death." The "Lake of Fire," commonly referred to as "Hell" is an actual place. It is a bottomless pit reserved for Satan, his followers, and those that have rejected the Saving Grace and the Power of Remission of sin by the shed Blood of Jesus Christ. The Bible refers to "Hell" as the "Second Death."

For years, I have pondered if man's soul is a part of the Spiritual "food-chain?" Is part of the value of man's soul related to the pleasures that demonic forces can derive from the horrid experiences that cause hurt and pain? Satan and his demonic forces frequently exploit men's souls. During an individual's lifetime, there are continual attempts, by the Devil, to injure and destroy them. During eternity, men's souls will be in an existence of torment; separated from God, in an eternal state of despair and total helplessness. Futility, without hope, and alienated from God forever. <u>No escape, no help, forever lost, and no chance to change their horrible existence</u>.

> WHAT A FEARFUL AND
> HORRIBLE EXISTENCE,
> NEVER TO ESCAPE
> WITH ALL IMAGINABLE
> TRAUMAS, HURTS, AND PAINS.
> A CONTINUAL STATE WITH
> NO POSSIBILITY OF HELP.
> DESPAIR AND HOPELESSNESS
> FOREVER AND EVER,
> <u>TIME WITHOUT END</u>
>
> WARNING! — ALARM!
> STOP! — DANGER!

QUESTION:

1. Do you believe these type of "death Experiences" should be shared? Yes___ No___ Explain your response.

_____

_____

_____

_____

_____

_____

2. If you have been a Christian for many years, at the present time, is there more or less emphasis on an Eternal Judgment? More___ Less___ What, in your opinion, are the reason(s)?

_____

_____

_____

_____

_____

3. Why must every individual ask God for forgiveness of their past and present sins? Briefly explain.

_____
_____
_____
_____
_____
_____

4. According to the Bible, what happens when an individual receives "Salvation?" "Salvation" is receiving the life of Jesus Christ personally and their sins being forgiven by His (Jesus') Blood. Briefly explain.

_____
_____
_____
_____
_____

WHAT TO DO:

Because individuals have not been instructed, they have no concept of the seriousness of "Eternal Death." Rarely are consequences espoused relating to "Eternal Damnation" and "Separation from God."

Each individual is responsible for their own salvation. God has made a "way of escape." — The "Lifeline of the BLOOD OF JESUS."

<u>The plan of salvation through the shed blood of Jesus Christ has made a "Way of Escape" for all of creation.</u>

DO NOT REJECT
THE <u>ONLY</u>
WAY OF ESCAPE!

Each individual will be judged before God. Forget popularity and public opinion. Seek and "accept" Jesus while you can. _Proverbs 28:5 states: Evil men understand not judgment: but they that seek the Lord understand all things._ Those that have not accepted JESUS CHRIST will appear and be judged at the Judgment Throne of God.

This world is so polluted and perverted. Popular opinion and public polls stifle the growth of many individuals. Frequently, individuals are too tolerant of other's opinions. Some are influenced and too timid to act upon what they believe God has said.

Accepting Christ is not to win a popularity contest. DO YOU WANT TO PLEASE GOD OR MAN? <u>Men's opinions and popularity change. GOD IS! God never changes; there is no variableness or turning in Him,</u> GOD IS ALWAYS THE SAME! *James 1:17 states: Every good gift and every perfect gift is from above, and cometh down from the Father of lights, with whom is no variableness, neither shadow of turning.*

SEEK AND "RUN"
AFTER GOD

MAN IS CORRUPT:

Man was given dominion, by God, over all of the earth. <u>*Genesis 1:26-28*</u>: *26. And God said, Let us make man in our image, after our likeness: and let them have dominion over the fish of the sea, and over the fowl of the air, and over the cattle, and <u>over all the earth</u>, and over every creeping thing that creepeth upon the earth. 27. So God created man in his own image, in the image of God created he him; male and female created he them. 28. And God blessed them, and God said unto them, Be fruitful, and multiply, and replenish the earth, and subdue it: and have dominion over the fish of the sea, and over the fowl of the air, and over every living thing that moveth upon the earth.*

Man has made a "mess" of this earth. He (man) has no regard of care for the species and the environment of earth. Consequently, the entire earth continues to be subjected to destructive issues because of man's lack of concern. His (man's) dominion (birthright) has been a "downfall" for the earth.

The Two Kingdoms Study Guide

This world consists of men that are liars, whose god is their belly and mind earthly things.

QUESTION:

5. Should Christians (followers of Christ) be more conscientious of the environment than other individuals? Yes___ No___ Explain your response.

_____
_____
_____
_____
_____

Philippians 3:18-19:

18. For many walk, of whom I have told you often, and now tell you even weeping, that they are the enemies of the cross of Christ: 19. Whose end is destruction, whose God is their belly, and whose glory is in their shame, who mind earthly things.

THESE MEN
ARE OF THEIR
FATHER THE DEVIL

If you desire to "follow" Jesus, the Holy Spirit will guide you. God has designed a specific purpose for your life. Ask God for His forgiveness and begin again. Even if you have tried many times, "get-up" and "try-again."

Begin to read the Bible. Begin in the book of John. Read the book of John over and over. Then, begin to read in Matthew, then Mark, and then Luke. Read the books of Matthew, Mark, Luke, and John until you truly understand the meanings contained in these books. Caution: DO NOT READ SO MUCH THAT YOU GET "BURNOUT." After you have read the books of Matthew, Mark, Luke, and John and understand these books, then turn your attention to other books of the Bible. Preferably the other books contained in the New Testament.

In addition, begin to spend time in prayer. Again, do not get "burnout." Maintain a consistent pattern of prayer that you can continually maintain. Do not listen to any other "inner voice" that does not agree with what you are reading in the Bible. Approach your "new-life" with the seriousness that an eternal decision deserves. All things have become new!

Ephesians 4:22-27:

22. That ye put off concerning the former conversation the old man, which is corrupt according to the deceitful lusts; 23. And be renewed in the spirit of your mind; 24. And that ye put on the new man, which after God is created in righteousness and true holiness. 25. Wherefore putting away lying, speak every man truth with his neighbour: for we are members one of another. 26. Be ye angry, and sin not: let not the sun go down upon your wrath: 27. Neither give place to the devil.

A NEW CREATION:

You have become a new creation. Old things have passed away.

II Corinthians 5:17-21:

17. Therefore if any man be in Christ, he is a new creature: old things are passed away; behold, all things are become new. 18. And all things are of God, who hath reconciled us to himself by Jesus Christ, and hath given to us the ministry of reconciliation; 19. To wit, that God was in Christ, reconciling the world unto himself, not imputing their trespasses unto them; and hath committed unto us the word of reconciliation. 20. Now then we are ambassadors for Christ, as though God did beseech you by us: we pray you in Christ's stead, be ye reconciled to God. 21. For he hath made him to be sin for us, who knew no sin; that we might be made the righteousness of God in him.

You are responsible for your own "Salvation." Seek out your "Salvation." In your heart, you hopefully sense and know the Truth. There is no need to debate or argue with other individuals regarding your beliefs. Waste no time with those that state, "I do not believe there is a God." By Biblical definition, such an individual is a "fool."

QUESTION:

6. What changes occur when an individual becomes a new "creation?" Briefly explain.

_____
_____
_____
_____
_____
_____

Psalms 14:1:

The fool hath said in his heart, There is no God. They are corrupt, they have done abominable works, there is none that doeth good. Psalms 53:1: The fool hath said in his heart, There is no God. Corrupt are they, and have done abominable iniquity: there is none that doeth good.

Additionally, the Bible instructs us, to <u>not</u> answer a "fool." _Proverbs 26:4: Answer not a fool according to his folly, lest thou also be like unto him._ The "fool" will not listen to others, because they believe they are right. _Proverbs 12:15: The way of the fool is right in his own eyes: but he that hearkeneth unto counsel is wise. Proverbs 23:9: Speak not in the ears of a fool: for he will despise the wisdom of thy words._ God, by his Word, says not to answer. It does not say to get angry, confused, frustrated, irritated, mean or worried. <u>JUST DON'T ANSWER</u>! (Silence is "Golden" during these moments.) Always attempt to live in "Peace" with all individuals. _Romans 12:18: If it be possible, as much as lieth in you, live peaceably with all men._ Do not be childish and reprimand or scold a "fool." These individuals ("fools") may be relatives, supposed friends, co-workers or strangers. Withdraw from these individuals as much as possible. Pray for them that they will become "enlightened." The prayers are to be prayed in the privacy of your personal "prayer closet," not in their presence.

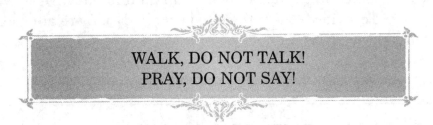

WALK, DO NOT TALK!
PRAY, DO NOT SAY!

Peace should always rule in our heart. Peace should be the umpire of our life. _Colossians 3:15: And let the peace of God rule in your hearts......_ Allow peace to rule in your life. As an umpire determines "ball" or "strike," let peace be the determining factor in each of life's decisions.

Remember:
PEACE OF MIND
NOT
PIECE OF MIND

QUESTION:

7. Why do you believe God calls an unbeliever of His (God's) existence a "fool?" Briefly explain.

_____

_____

_____

_____

_____

_____

8. What evidence, in your opinion, exists to "believe" in God? Briefly explain.

_____

_____

_____

_____

_____

_____

9. Have you observed individuals involved in an unproductive conversation attempting to convince others that God exists? Briefly relate one of these situations.

_____

_____

_____

_____

_____

_____

ENTROPY:

Elements rust, corrode, decay, and return to their base components. This "return" to base components is referred to as "entropy." There is no need to "debate" or "argue" the Theory of Evolution and the Theory of Creation. I believe little can be said or done to change an individual's belief regarding these issues. It is what God says that is important, not what any "person" proclaims. "Debating" or "arguing" the Theory of Evolution and the Theory of Creation is analogous, to me, of two (2) small children in a sandbox throwing sand at each other. <u>Both individuals are childish and remain in the "mental-sandbox," not resolving the issue.</u>

QUESTION:

10. Why is it so futile (hopeless) to debate the Theory of Evolution and the Theory of Creation? Briefly explain.

_____

_____

_____

_____

_____

_____

The Watchmaker
A poem by Dave Hawkins

A long time ago on a planet so bare,
Some water and dirt got mixed up with the air.
Some sand and some rocks to make it just right,
The stage was all set in the deep of the night.

A bolt of white lightning, a great peal of thunder,
And suddenly, there was a marvelous wonder.
The rocks yielded metal, the sand turned to glass,
And as the years flew, a new thing came to pass.

The metal formed gears, the glass a watch face,
And little by little, things fell into place.
The parts came together, just like a good rhyme,
With ticks and with tocks and with hands that tell time.
A beautiful watch began ticking one day,
Formed all by itself in a wonderful way.

"Ridiculous story!" you say with a grin.
"Impossible, laughable... surely a sin!
A watch needs a watchmaker, that's plain to see.
A designer and builder that makes it for me."

Now all life is made of some interesting stuff,
Cells of all shapes like blobs filled with fluff.
But looks are deceiving and what we find there.
Are factories and highways and gadgets to spare.

Assembly lines, robots, electrical cable,
Libraries, software; just look, if you're able.
The marvels we see with a microscope's stare.
Make a watch look so simple, we dare not compare.

Now the doctor from Oxford say cells came by Chance.
From God down to You in a beautiful dance.
What's wrong with their thinking to have such odd notions?
That cells could just happen from dirt and warm oceans!

A cell and its wonders amaze all who see.
And a cell, like a watch, by Chance cannot be.
Those cells can build hummingbirds, agile and free,
Bumble bees, snails, my backyard oak tree.

A woodpecker built with a jackhammer nose?
Lightning bugs, monkeys, a beautiful rose,
And beetles with bombs that give frogs a surprise.
Chameleons with camouflage and some weird eyes.

All nature on Earth is so perfectly fine,
We have to admit that its all by Design,
And our Maker owns everything both great and small.
He's the masterful "Watchmaker," Lord over all.

SESSION FOUR:

LIFE AND DEATH

Read Pages: 36-52 of the book entitled "Two Kingdoms."

INCEPTION OF LIFE:

Inception of life began for Adam when God breathed into him and he became a "living soul." Genesis 2:7: *And the Lord God formed man of the dust of the ground, and breathed into his nostrils the breath of life; and man became a living soul.* Sufficient life was given to cause the immortality of man's soul.

After the death and resurrection of JESUS, He appears to His disciples and He "breathed" on them, and said, "Receive ye the Holy Ghost."

John 20:19-22:

19. Then the same day at evening, being the first day of the week, when the doors were shut where the disciples were assembled for fear of the Jews, came Jesus and stood in the midst, and saith unto them, Peace be unto you. 20. And when he had so said, he shewed unto them his hands and his side. Then were the disciples glad, when they saw the Lord. 21. Then said Jesus to them again, Peace be unto you: as my Father hath sent me, even so send I you. 22. And when he had said this, he breathed on them, and saith unto them, Receive ye the Holy Ghost:

JESUS breathes life into the immortal souls of his disciples and they receive the Spiritual breath of Jesus. Paul explains this "quickening of the spirit" in *I Corinthians 15:45: And so it is written, the first man Adam was made a living soul; the last Adam was made a quickening spirit.*

The initial breath, from God, causing man to become a "living soul," now becomes a vast explosive igniting of man's spirit. The Light of God, through Jesus, infinitely expands man's soul and "spirit-life." The flicker of light and life in man's soul explodes and man becomes a new creation. Out of the belly, should flow "Rivers of Living Water." When talking with the Samaritan woman at the well, Jesus tells her that she could receive a well of water springing up into everlasting life.

John 4:10-14:

10. Jesus answered and said unto her, If thou knewest the gift of God, and who it is that saith to thee, Give me to drink; thou wouldest have asked of him, and he would have given thee living water. 11. The woman saith unto him, Sir, thou hast nothing to draw with, and the well is deep; from whence then hast thou that living water? 12. Art thou greater than our father Jacob, which gave us the well, and drank thereof himself, and his children, and his cattle? 13. Jesus answered and said unto her, Whosoever drinketh of this water shall thirst again: 14. But whosoever drinketh of this water that I shall give him shall never thirst; but the water that I shall give him shall be in him a well of water springing up into everlasting life.

NEW BIRTH:

Until the Holy Spirit breathes upon man's soul, man's soul will continue to be in a "lost" state. Man will remain eternally alienated and out of the presence of God, "out of the garden." The alienation is referring to Adam and Eve being expelled (kicked out or driven away) and excluded from the Garden of Eden after their disobedience.

Genesis 3:23-24:

23. Therefore the Lord God sent him forth from the garden of Eden, to till the ground from whence he was taken. 24. So he drove out the man; and he placed at the east of the garden of Eden Cherubims, and a flaming sword which turned every way, to keep the way of the tree of life.

QUESTION:

1. What occurs when an individual is "reborn" (experiences a "new birth," in Christ Jesus)? Briefly explain.

_____

_____

_____

_____

Of course, God knew that Adam and Eve would disobey and fail. In fact, had they never "failed" (disobeyed), there would only be Kings and Priests upon the Earth in an "Earthly Kingdom." Now, through JESUS CHRIST, we can become Kings and Priests in a "Heavenly Kingdom." There is now the potential for individuals to become a part of the "Bride of Christ." *Revelation 1:6: And hath made us kings and priests unto God and his Father; to him be glory and dominion for ever and ever. Amen.*

If the Spirit of God leads us, we have become adopted by God and are the Sons of God. As children of God, we become heirs of God if we suffer with Christ.

Romans 8:14-21:

14. For as many as are led by the Spirit of God, they are the sons of God. 15. For ye have not received the spirit of bondage again to fear; but ye have received the Spirit of adoption, whereby we cry, Abba, Father. 16. The Spirit itself beareth witness with our spirit, that we are the children of God. 17. And if children, and joint-heirs with Christ; if so be that we suffer with him, that we may be also glorified together. 18. For I reckon that the sufferings of this present time are not worthy to be compared with the glory which shall be revealed in us. 19. For the earnest expectation of the creature waiteth for the manifestation of the sons of God. 20. For the creature was made subject to vanity, not willingly, but by reason of him who hath subjected the same in hope. 21. Because the creature itself also shall be delivered from the bondage of corruption into the glorious liberty of the children of God.

Christ (the last Adam) was made a quickening spirit. *I Corinthians 15:45: And so it is written, The first man Adam was made a living soul; the last*

Adam was made a quickening spirit." The members of The "Kingdom of God" become recipients of "Eternal Life." "Eternal Life" is explained later in this Study Guide. (See page 53 for the topic relating to "Eternal Life," and page 59 for the topic entitled "Born of God.")

QUESTION:

2. If Adam and Eve had never disobeyed (sinned), would there have been a need for Jesus to come to the Earth? Yes___ No___ Briefly explain your response.

_____

_____

_____

_____

_____

_____

3. Why are those that have accepted Jesus in a "higher" position than Adam and Eve were even before their (Adam and Eve's) disobedience (sin)? Briefly explain.

_____

_____

_____

_____

_____

4. Mankind was not cursed when expelled from the Garden of Eden. Paul expresses a great mystery in *Ephesians 5:30-32. 30. For we are members of his body, of his flesh, and of his bones. 31. For this cause shall a man leave his father and mother, and shall be joined unto his wife, and they two shall be one flesh. 32. This is a great mystery: but I speak concerning Christ and the church.* Briefly describe the potential of mankind becoming a member of the Bride of Christ.

_____

_____

_____

_____

_____

_____

5. As a husband and wife become one flesh, do you believe Paul is speaking this mystery and relates that as marital relationships grow, there is an eternity for growth with Christ? Yes___ No___ Briefly explain.

_____

_____

_____

_____

_____

_____

MAN IS BANISHED FROM GOD'S PRESENCE:

Notice in Genesis 3:14-21, as God dictates Justice, man is banished from God's Presence. He (man) is expelled (kicked-out or driven away) and excluded from the Garden (The presence of God). Man's punishment for disobedience is being driven away from God's Presence. At that time, the edict of God no longer allowed man to have intimate harmonious communication with Him. The serpent is cursed in Genesis 3:14. The ground (earth), from which man came, is cursed in Genesis 3:17, but man's punishment is banishment from God's Presence.

Genesis 3:14-24:

14. And the Lord said unto the serpent, Because thou hast done this, thou art cursed above all cattle, and above every beast of the field; upon thy belly shalt thou go, and dust shalt thou eat all the days of thy life: 15. And I will put enmity between thee and the woman, and between thy seed and her seed; it shall bruise thy head, and thou shalt bruise his heel. 16. Unto the woman he said, I will greatly multiply thy sorrow and thy conception; in sorrow thou shalt bring forth children; and thy desire shall be to thy husband, and he shall rule over thee. 17. And unto Adam he said, Because thou hast hearkened unto the voice of thy wife, and hast eaten of the tree, of which I commanded thee, saying, Thou shalt not eat of it: cursed is the ground for thy sake; in sorrow shalt thou eat of it all the days of thy life; 18. Thorns also and thistles shall it bring forth to thee; and thou shalt eat the herb of the field; 19. In the sweat of thy face shalt thou eat bread, till thou return unto the ground; for out of it wast thou taken: for dust thou art, and unto dust shalt thou return. 20. And Adam called his wife's name Eve, because she was the mother of all living. 21. Unto Adam also and to his wife did the Lord God make coats of skins, and clothed them. 22. And the Lord God said, Behold, the man is become as one of us, to know good and evil: and now, lest he put forth his hand, and take also of the tree of life, and eat, and live for ever: 23. Therefore the Lord God sent him forth from the garden of Eden, to till the ground from whence he was taken. 24. So he drove out the man; and he placed at the east of the garden of Eden Cherubims, and a flaming sword which turned every way, to keep the way of the tree of life.

CREATION OF THE EARTH:

Before creation of the earth, "darkness" covered the earth. Genesis 1:2: And the earth was without form, and void; and darkness was upon the face of the deep. And the Spirit of God moved upon the face of the waters. God then declares: "let there be Light" and there was Light.

Genesis 1:3-4:

3. And God said, Let there be light: and there was light. 4. And God saw the light, that it was good: and God divided the light from the darkness.

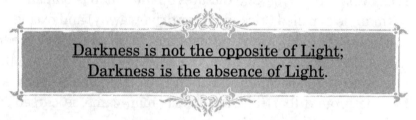

Darkness is not the opposite of Light;
Darkness is the absence of Light.

CREATION OF MAN:

Man was created from the earth. *Genesis 2:7: And the Lord God formed man of the dust of the ground, and breathed into his nostrils the breath of life; and man became a living soul.* God planted a garden and then placed man, whom he had formed, in the garden. *Genesis 2:8: And the Lord God planted a garden eastward in Eden; and there he put the man whom he had formed.* When man was expelled from the garden, he was alienated from the presence of God. The beauty and fellowship of God was no longer available to him (man). Until Jesus came and sacrificed His Life's Blood as Atonement for all sin, man's soul was covered with "darkness." Until the "Rebirth" of man's soul, and man becomes a "quickening spirit," man's soul remains in "darkness." The "Rebirth" occurs by accepting Jesus and His Saving Grace through the shedding of His Blood on the Cross-of Calvary. In the Bible, "Rebirth," is also referred to as "Born of God."

TWO OPTIONS:

I. TWO BIRTHS AND ONE DEATH
OR
II. ONE BIRTH AND TWO DEATHS

EARTHLY BIRTH:

All individuals have an earthly birth. They are born of their parents and have a flicker of life that was initially breathed into the soul of man. Again, *Genesis 2:7: And the Lord God formed man of the dust of the ground, and breathed into his nostrils the breath of life; and man became a living soul.*

EARTHLY DEATH:

Eventually, each individual will have a natural death. *Hebrews 9:27: And it is appointed unto men once to die, but after this the judgment.*

ETERNAL DEATH:

Eternal death is based solely upon the acceptance or non-acceptance of Jesus Christ as a personal Saviour. If we do not accept Jesus, we will remain alienated and separated eternally from God.

ETERNAL LIFE:

After the judgment, at the Great White Throne of God, Revelation 20:11, those whose names are written in the "Book of Life" are received into a New Heaven. For those "Born of God," there will be an Eternal Life of Enjoyment in the "Kingdom of God." What an exciting Eternity for the heirs to the "Kingdom of God."

Revelation, Chapters 21 and 22, makes clear the eternal transpiring for individuals in the Two Kingdoms. Those that have lived according to the "Kingdom of This World" are further described in Revelation 22:15: *For without are dogs, and sorcerers, and whoremongers, and murderers, and idolaters, and whosoever loveth and maketh a lie.* Additionally, those that have lived according to the "Kingdom of This World" are described in Revelation 21:8: *But the fearful, and unbelieving, and the abominable, and murderers, and whoremongers, and sorcerers, and idolaters, and all liars, shall have their part in the lake which burneth with fire and brimstone: which is the second death.* (There will be no entrance into the City of God for these individuals.)

Revelation, Chapters 21 and 22, indicates, in detail, the division of The Two Kingdoms.

Revelation Chapter 21:

1. And I saw a new heaven and a new earth: for the first heaven and the first earth were passed away; and there was no more sea. 2. And I John saw the holy city, new Jerusalem, coming down from God out of heaven, prepared as a bride adorned for her husband. 3. And I heard a great voice out of heaven saying, Behold, the tabernacle of God is with men, and he will dwell with them, and they shall be his people, and God himself shall be with them, and be their God. 4. And God shall wipe away all tears from their eyes; and there shall be no more death, neither sorrow, nor crying, neither shall there be any more pain: for the former things are passed away. 5. And he that sat upon the throne said, Behold, I make all things new. And he said unto me, Write: for these words are true and faithful. 6. And he said unto me, It is done. I am Alpha and Omega, the beginning and the end. I will give unto him that is athirst of the fountain of the water of life freely. 7. He that overcometh shall inherit all things; and I will be his God, and he shall be my son. 8. But the fearful, and unbelieving, and the abominable, and murderers, and whoremongers, and sorcerers, and idolaters, and all liars, shall have their part in the lake which burneth with fire and brimstone: which is the second death. 9. And there came unto me one of the seven angels which had the seven vials full of the seven last plagues, and talked with me, saying, Come hither, I will shew thee the bride, the Lamb's wife. 10. And he carried me away in the spirit to a great and high mountain, and shewed me that great city, the holy Jerusalem, descending out of heaven from God. 11. Having the glory of God: and her light was like unto a stone most precious, even like a jasper stone, clear as crystal; 12. And had a wall great and high, and had twelve gates, and at the gates twelve angels, and names written thereon, which are the names of the twelve tribes of the children of Israel: 13. On the east three gates; on the north three gates; on the south three gates; and on the west three gates. 14. And the wall of the city had twelve foundations, and in them the names of the twelve apostles of the Lamb. 15. And he that talked with me had a golden reed to measure the city, and the gates thereof, and the wall thereof. 16. And the city lieth four-square, and the length is as large as the breadth: and he measured the city with the reed, twelve thousand furlongs. The length and the breadth and the height of it are equal. 17. And he measured the wall thereof, an hundred and forty and four cubits, according to the measure of a man, that is, of the angel. 18. And the building of the wall of it was of jasper: and the city was pure gold, like unto clear glass. 19. And the foundations of the wall of the city were garnished with all manner of precious stones. The first foundation was jasper; the second, sapphire; the third, a chalcedony; the fourth, an emerald; 20. The fifth, sardonyx; the sixth, sardius; the seventh, chrysolite; the eighth, beryl; the ninth, a topaz; the tenth, a chrysoprasus; the eleventh, a jacinth; the twelfth, an amethyst. 21. And the twelve gates were twelve pearls; every several gate was of one pearl: and the street of the city was pure gold, as it were transparent glass. 22. And I saw no temple therein: for the Lord God Almighty and the Lamb are the temple of it. 23. And the city had

The Two Kingdoms Study Guide

no need of the sun, neither of the moon, to shine in it: for the glory of God did lighten it, and the Lamb is the light thereof. 24. And the nations of them which are saved shall walk in the light of it: and the kings of the earth do bring their glory and honour into it. 25. And the gates of it shall not be shut at all by day: for there shall be no night there. 26. And they shall bring the glory and honour of the nations into it. 27. And there shall in no wise enter into it any thing that defileth, neither whatsoever worketh abomination, or maketh a lie: but they which are written in the Lamb's book of life.

Revelation Chapter 22:

1. And he shewed me a pure river of water of life, clear as crystal, proceeding out of the throne of God and of the Lamb. 2. In the midst of the street of it, and on either side of the river, was there the tree of life, which bare twelve manner of fruits, and yielded her fruit every month: and the leaves of the tree were for the healing of the nations. 3. And there shall be no more curse: but the throne of God and of the Lamb shall be in it; and his servants shall serve him: 4. And they shall see his face; and his name shall be in their foreheads. 5. And there shall be no night there; and they need no candle, neither light of the sun; for the Lord God giveth them light: and they shall reign for ever and ever. 6. And he said unto me, These sayings are faithful and true: and the Lord God of the holy prophets sent his angel to shew unto his servants the things which must shortly be done. 7. Behold, I come quickly: blessed is he that keepeth the sayings of the prophecy of this book. 8. And I John saw these things, and heard them. And when I had heard and seen, I fell down to worship before the feet of the angel which shewed me these things. 9. Then saith he unto me, See thou do it not: for I am thy fellowservant, and of thy brethren the prophets, and of them which keep the sayings of this book: worship God. 10. And he saith unto me, Seal not the sayings of the prophecy of this book: for the time is at hand. 11. He that is unjust, let him be unjust still: and he which is filthy, let him be filthy still; and he that is righteous, let him be righteous still: and he that is holy, let him be holy still. 12. And, behold, I come quickly; and my reward is with me, to give every man according as his work shall be. 13. I am Alpha and Omega, the beginning and the end, the first and the last. 14. Blessed are they that do his commandments, that they may have right to the tree of life, and may enter in through the gates into the city. 15. For without are dogs, and sorcerers, and whoremongers, and murderers, and idolaters, and whosoever loveth and maketh a lie. 16. I Jesus have sent mine angel to testify unto you these things in the churches. I am the root of the offspring of David, and the bright and morning star. 17. And the Spirit and the bride say, Come. And let him that heareth say, Come. And let him that is athirst come. And whosoever will, let him take the water of life

freely. 18. For I testify unto every man that heareth the words of the prophecy of this book, If any man shall add unto these things, God shall add unto him the plagues that are written in this book: 19. And if any man shall take away from the words of the book of this prophecy, God shall take away his part out of the book of life, and out of the holy city, and from the things which are written in this book. 20. He which testifieth these things saith, Surely I come quickly. Amen. Even so, come, Lord Jesus. 21. The grace of our Lord Jesus Christ be with you all. Amen.

TWO OPTIONS:

OPTION ONE:

TWO BIRTHS AND ONE DEATH:
1. Earthly Birth
2. Eternal Birth
And
1. Earthly Death

OPTION TWO:

ONE BIRTH AND TWO DEATHS:
1. Earthly Birth
And
1. Earthly Death
2. Eternal Death

EXPLANATION OF ETERNAL DEATH:

The disciples were being persecuted and Jesus comforts them with words of encouragement. Jesus stated to not fear those who can kill the body, but fear Him (God) who can destroy both the soul and body. *Matthew 10:28: And fear not them which kill the body, but are not able to kill the soul: but rather fear him which is able to destroy both soul and body in hell.*

An individual receives a "joining" of body and soul (life) when their earthly life begins. Eternal death will begin, for those not "Born Again," when the body and soul of a man is reunited at the Judgment Throne of God.

QUESTION:

6. Briefly explain "Eternal Death."

_____

_____

_____

_____

_____

_____

EXPLANATION OF MAN'S SOUL AND BODY:

1. The soul of man receives life from God.
2. The body receives life from the soul.

At man's physical death, the body no longer has capacity to contain the soul. At physical death, the soul and body are separated. Therefore, natural and earthly death has occurred.

If an individual has not been "Born of God," there is awaiting a "Second Death." This "Second Death" will occur when the body and soul are reunited and Judged by God at His Throne of Judgment. This is what Jesus meant when He stated, "Do not fear those that can kill the body, but rather fear God who can destroy both body and soul."

Because God's Breath is immortal (eternal), and God breathed into man, he became a living soul. Thus, each living soul is immortal (man's soul is eternal).

FINAL JUDGMENT:

When the "reuniting" of the body and soul occurs at the Judgment Throne of God, God will pronounce His Final Judgment. (Revelation 20:11-15) Those individuals that have not accepted His Plan of Salvation (ACCEPTING JESUS CHRIST AS THEIR LORD AND SAVIOUR BY THE BLOOD OF JESUS) will be banished eternally from His (God's) presence. Individuals that have not accepted Jesus Christ, as their Lord and Saviour, are also referred to as "Lost" or "Damned Souls."

Although the flicker of light in their soul will eternally exist, their existence is said to be "death," rather than "life." These souls will exist in a horrid and tormented state. The souls of individuals that have not been "Born of God," will be banished from God to an eternal punishment.

Revelation 20:11-15:

11. And I saw a great white throne, and him that sat on it, from whose face the earth and the heaven fled away; and there was found no place for them. 12. And I saw the dead, small and great, stand before God; and the books were opened: and another book was opened, which is the book of life: and the dead were judged out of those things which were written in the books, according to their works. 13. And the sea gave up the dead which were in it; and death and hell delivered up the dead which were in them: and they were judged every man according to their works. 14. And death and hell were cast into the lake of fire. This is the second death. 15. And whosoever was not found written in the book of life was cast into the lake of fire.

QUESTION:

7. Discuss the correlations between Adam and Eve being expelled (banished) from the Garden of Eden, and individuals being expelled (banished) eternally from God's Presence.

_____

_____

_____

_____

_____

GOD WANTS YOU:

God's desire is that all would come to repentance and accept His Plan of Salvation. His desire is that no one would perish.

II Peter 3:9-15:

9. The Lord is not slack concerning his promise, as some men count slackness; but is longsuffering to us-ward, not willing that any should perish, but that all should come to repentance. 10. But the day of the Lord will come as a thief in the night; in the which the heavens shall pass away with a great noise, and the elements shall melt with fervent heat, the earth also and the works that are therein shall be burned up. 11. Seeing then that all these things shall be dissolved, what manner of persons ought ye to be in all holy conversation and godliness, 12. Looking for and hasting unto the coming of the day of God, wherein the heavens being on fire shall be dissolved, and the elements shall melt with fervent heat? 13. Nevertheless we, according to his promise, look for new heavens and a new earth, wherein dwelleth righteousness. 14. Wherefore, beloved, seeing that ye look for such things, be diligent that ye may be found of him in peace, without spot, and blameless. 15. And account that the longsuffering of our Lord is salvation; even as our beloved brother Paul also according to the wisdom given unto him hath written unto you;

In addition, one of the most quoted scriptures denoting that God is not willing that any would perish is John 3:16. However, verse 15 and 17 are seldom quoted.

John 3:15-17:

15. That whosoever believeth in him should not perish, but have eternal life. 16. For God so loved the world, that he gave his only begotten Son, that whosoever believeth in him should not perish, but have everlasting life. 17. For God sent not his Son into the world to condemn the world; but that the world through him might be saved.

BORN OF GOD:

Jesus shed His Blood on the "Cross of Calvary" and His Blood cleanses from all unrighteousness. *I John 1:9: If we confess our sins, he is faithful and just to forgive us our sins, and to cleanse us from all unrighteousness.* If an individual confesses their sin(s) and accepts Jesus Christ, their soul is "Reborn." Again, this "Rebirth" is called "Born of God." Jesus' Blood cleanses us from all sin and we become a "New Creation." In Christian-terminology, "New Creation" is also referred to as: "Rebirth," "Saved," "New Creature," "Born Again," or "Born of God."

If we truly have been "Born of God," we will cease to commit sin. *I John 3:9: Whosoever is born of God doth not commit sin; for his seed remaineth in him: and he cannot sin, because he is born of God.* John, in the next verse, declares that not committing sin is how the children of God are manifest. In other words, this is the litmus test. Are you a child of God, or are you a child of the devil? *I John 3:10: In this the children of God are manifest, and the children of the devil: whosoever doeth not righteousness is not of God, neither he that loveth not his brother.* If we continue to sin, a "Rebirth" into God's Kingdom never transpired. This is very clearly stated! <u>Again, for emphasis, I restate the Bible verses</u>.

I John 3:9-10:

9. Whosoever is born of God doth not commit sin; for his seed remaineth in him: and he cannot sin, because he is born of God. 10. In this the children of God are manifest, and the children of the devil: whosoever doeth not righteousness is not of God, neither he that loveth not his brother.

PERSONAL RESPONSIBILITY:

Each individual is responsible to "work-out" their own Salvation. Seek this with fear and trembling. *Philippians 2:12: Wherefore, my beloved, as ye have always obeyed, not as in my presence only, but now much more in my absence, work out your own salvation with fear and trembling.*

Many individuals live "defeated" lives, because the explosive dynamic "Rebirthing" has never transpired in their personal life. They have taken someone's advice and actually believe they are "Born of God." *Again, if you are "Born of God," you will cease from sin.*

For your personal eternal spiritual existence, read, again, I John 3:9-10: *Allow God to speak for Himself.*

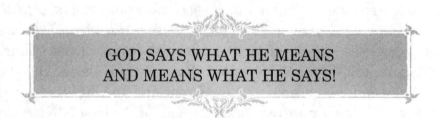

GOD SAYS WHAT HE MEANS
AND MEANS WHAT HE SAYS!

QUESTION:

8. Do you believe it is possible for an individual to live a life "free from sin?" Yes___ No___ Briefly explain.

_____

_____

_____

_____

_____

_____

SESSION FIVE:

LACK OF FORGIVENESS

Read Pages: 53-60 of the book entitled "Two Kingdoms."

DEPRESSION:

Depression is common and a concern for many individuals. It is a topic that seems to be avoided. Depression affects and effects most individuals during their life. Major causes are: health, medication(s), emotional injury, loneliness, anger, negativism, hatred and other dysfunctional psychological emotions, narcissism (love of self), lack of control, and lack of forgiveness.

The cycle of Depression is: (1) Anxiety, Frustration, and Irritation; (2) Anger; (3) Depression. (After anger occurs, depression follows within a few hours to a few days.)

Our enemy, the Devil, is quick to accuse and desires individuals to become ashamed of their actions and frustrated with their life. (Thus, the cycle of Irritation, Anger, and Depression often repeats for some individuals.)

Once a psychological habit has been formed, it is difficult to change behavioral patterns. Hopefully, in this section of the book, insights will be written to assist in the alleviation of depression.

QUESTION:

1. Have you observed a pattern or cycle of behavior that predicts depressive behavior in individuals? Yes___ No___ If yes, briefly explain.

_____

_____

_____

_____

_____

_____

2. Do you believe some individuals just choose to be depressed for attention? Yes___ No___ Briefly explain your response.

_____

_____

_____

_____

_____

LACK OF FORGIVENESS:

Lack of Forgiveness seems to be a major cause of depression and dementia. Some individuals have great difficulty forgiving, even forgiving those closest to them. At this time, I think of a friend. She could not forgive her husband for an infidelity, he committed, early in their marriage. She was constantly frustrated and oscillated between being nice and angry. Even though a seemingly good Christian, she was tormented by sometimes cursing and swearing. She took counsel regarding this situation. About seven (7) or eight (8) years ago, she had an opportunity to forgive and "move-on" with her life; she virtually refused. Within twelve (12) to eighteen (18) months, she suffered from dementia and is now close to "full-blown" Alzheimer's. In the elderly, I frequently see dementia and Alzheimer's. According to studies, there are numerous causes of dementia and Alzheimer's. I believe one of the causes is Lack of Forgiveness. Lack of Forgiveness seems to emotionally destroy an individual.

The unresolved situation takes more and more of the individual's mental time. There seems to be an involuntary mechanism for "mental self-preservation." If an individual does not take control of their emotional stress and traumas, for emotional and mental survival, the mind begins to "shut-down." Ultimately, mental confusion ensues and disorientation begins. Forgetfulness of names, locations, and events become more pronounced.

Lack of Forgiveness and Depression affects an individual's personality. I worked with an individual for over thirty (30) years; he could not forgive his wife. He refused to retire because his wife would then receive a portion of his retirement. Their agreement was, at retirement, she would receive a portion of his retirement. She would receive no monies until he retired. He worked until he had a stroke. This individual maintained he was a Christian. He did numerous good things for the Christian Community, but he continued to suffer from emotional difficulties. He seemed to have a split personality. Sometimes he was very congenial and at other times, he was not "fun" to be around. He had a temper; was very negative at times; and prided himself in being the "devil's advocate."— (his term.) Sadly, today, he is still suffering from partial paralysis and unable to travel or do those things he wanted to do during his retirement. Although he has a very good financial income and stability, he cannot enjoy life. Claiming Christianity, but still angry and does not want to talk to those he knows. I contacted him numerous times, but he did not want to talk or get together. His statement was "I will call you back." <u>HIS SITUATION FORCED HIM INTO SECLUSION AND ISOLATION</u>.

QUESTION:

3. What does lack of forgiveness cause in the lives of individuals? Briefly describe.

_____

_____

_____

_____

_____

4. Describe a situation of an individual you know that had difficulties forgiving.

_____

_____

_____

_____

_____

_____

Matthew Chapter 18:23-35:

23. Therefore is the kingdom of heaven likened unto a certain king, which would take account of his servants. 24. And when he had begun to reckon, one was brought unto him, which owed him ten thousand talents. 25. But forasmuch as he had not to pay, his lord commanded him to be sold, and his wife, and children, and all that he had, and payment to be made. 26. The servant therefore fell down, and worshipped him, saying, Lord, have patience with me, and I will pay thee all. 27. Then the lord of that servant was moved with compassion, and loosed him, and forgave him the debt. 28. But the same servant went out, and found one of his fellowservants, which owed him an hundred pence: and he laid hands on him, and took him by the throat, saying, Pay me that thou owest. 29. And his fellowservant fell down at his feet, and besought him, saying, Have patience with me, and I will pay thee all. 30. And he would not: but went and cast him into prison, till he should pay the debt. 31. So when his fellowservants saw what was done, they were very sorry, and came and told unto their lord all that was done. 32. Then his lord, after that he had called him, said unto him, O thou wicked servant, I forgave thee all that debt, because thou desiredst me: 33. Shouldest not thou also have had compassion on thy fellowservant, even as I had pity on thee? 34. And his lord was wroth, and delivered him to the tormentors, till he should pay all that was due unto him. 35. So likewise shall my heavenly Father do also unto you, if ye from your hearts forgive not every one his brother their trespasses.

If we do not forgive others, God does not forgive us. The tenderness that God shows us is directly proportional to the tenderness that we show to others. We can either have "Justice" or "Mercy."

James 5:13-15:

13. Is any among you afflicted? Let him pray. Is any merry? Let him sing psalms. 14. Is any sick among you? let him call for the elders of the church;

and let them pray over him, anointing him with oil in the name of the Lord: 15. And the prayer of faith shall save the sick, and the Lord shall raise him up; and if he have committed sins, they shall be forgiven him.

Notice in James 5:13, that if an individual is "afflicted," they are to pray. Individuals with depression and mental torment want others to pray, when James states for them to pray. (James states a difference between affliction and sickness.)

Tormentors are evil spirits that attack an individual's mind and emotions. Tormentors are related to mental torment. The word "afflicted" refers to a mental "affliction," not a physical "affliction." Lack of Forgiveness releases tormentors into an individual's life.

QUESTION:

5. Briefly explain the personal responsibilities of individuals to maintain their mental health.

_____

_____

_____

_____

_____

_____

Lack of Forgiveness includes Forgiveness of Self. For some individuals, it is more difficult to forgive themselves, than to forgive others. Some individuals are anguished by poor decisions they have made in the past. These decisions may include, but not limited to: poor financial decisions, poor marital decisions, poor moral decisions, poor job decisions, not continuing in school, and many other poor decisions. Forgive yourself and "move-on" in life. If there is some way to change the situation, do it. If there is nothing you can do, cease from the thought(s) of poor previous decisions and acts. Never say "Oh, God cannot forgive me, I've gone too far." You have an advocate. God has said in *I John 2:1: My little children, these things write I unto you, that ye sin not. And if any man sin, we have an advocate with the Father, Jesus Christ the righteous:* Actually, if we deny that God can forgive us, excepting for blasphemy of the Holy Spirit (Calling God's Spirit Evil), we make God a teller of untruths. God is not a liar, but every man is a liar. God is with the humble of heart, not the "macho" attitude displayed by some individuals. God lifts up the humble, but "puts down" those that try to lift themselves up.

James 4:10: Humble yourselves in the sight of the Lord, and he shall lift you up. James 4:6: But he giveth more grace. Wherefore he saith, God resisteth the proud, but giveth grace unto the humble.

QUESTION:

6. Why do you believe some individuals have more difficulty forgiving themselves than forgiving others? Briefly explain.

_____
_____
_____
_____
_____
_____

The answer to Depression is The JOY OF THE LORD. Music releases tension associated with the soul and spirit. *James 5:13: Any merry, let* <u>*him*</u> *sing.* Not others sing, but let <u>him</u> sing. King Saul was "soothed" (comforted) by David's singing. However, he only enjoyed temporary reliefs, from his torments, rather than a continued relief. David was called into King Saul's presence to play his (David's) harp and Saul's depression would be lifted. However, the oppression and depression was only temporarily relieved and King Saul would revert to his negative state of mind. (I Samuel 19:9) Saul has killed his thousands, but David has killed his tens of thousands. What a difference between the Saul of the Old Testament and the Saul of the New Testament. Both of the tribe of Benjamin; King Saul's stature (head and shoulders above others) got him his position. Saul (Paul) was humbled on the Road to Damascus and became humble and obedient during his lifetime. Saul's name was ultimately changed to Paul, indicating a vast transformation of his life and character.

Depression causes an individual to be non-effective in their personal life and their Spiritual life. Their Christian witness is negatively affected. If we are not joyous, as Christians, who wants to be like us? The "world" looks for happiness in some entertainment venue, rather than seeing and following after Christians. Joy should spring from our "inner-being" and flow like "Living Waters." David in Psalm 51 declares Joy is the secret to teach transgressors the "Way of the Lord," and sinners to be converted.

Psalms 51:10-13:

10. Create in me a clean heart, O God; and renew a right spirit within me.
11. Cast me not away from thy presence; and take not thy holy spirit from me.
12. Restore unto me the joy of thy salvation; and uphold me with thy free

spirit. 13. Then will I teach transgressors thy ways; and sinners shall be converted unto thee.

Shallowness of Communication defeats our Joy. In our society and lives, it is difficult to remain "fixed" and "determined" upon our objectives. (Both Natural and Spiritual, especially the Spiritual.) Individuals can read the scripture, but it may not affect their spirit and change their life. Jesus expressed this to Peter when He asked him if he loved Him. Jesus asked Peter three (3) times if he loved him. (Do you love me, yes; do you love me; yes. do you love me; yes.)

John 21:15-17:

15. So when they had dined, Jesus saith to Simon Peter, Simon, son of Jonas, lovest thou me more than these? He saith unto him, Yea, Lord; thou knowest that I love thee. He saith unto him, Feed my lambs. 16. He saith to him again the second time, Simon, son of Jonas, lovest thou me? He saith unto him, Yea, Lord; thou knowest that I love thee. He saith unto him, Feed my sheep. 17. He saith unto him the third time, Simon, son of Jonas, lovest thou me? And he said unto him, Lord, thou knowest all things; thou knowest that I love thee. Jesus saith unto him, Feed my sheep.

Jesus gives us a "key" to a successful life: become "other-oriented," rather than "self-oriented." (Feed my lambs; Feed my sheep.) <u>Helping others gets us off our own difficulties and allows us to focus externally</u>.

Much communication seems to be shallow, trivial, nonsensical and trite. Some individuals would rather tell a brief joke than talk of life and eternal issues.

PRAYER:

Father, we ask that your continued presence of life and the Holy Spirit be with us and guide us continually. There is Great Joy and Life in your presence. Overshadow and fulfill in us what you want us to be. May we be quick to do your will. Let us assist those around us. May we always be kind and gentle. Deliver us from all "Evil." Our Father which art in Heaven, Hallowed be thy name, thy Kingdom Come, thy will be done on Earth as it is in Heaven. Give us this day, our daily bread and forgive us our debts as we forgive our debtors. And Lead us not into temptation, but deliver us from Evil, for Thine is the Kingdom; and the Power, and the Glory forever, Amen.

QUESTION:

7. Do you believe the "offender" (the individual that caused the hurt) can do anything to shorten the time it takes the "offended" (the individual that was hurt) to work through their hurt and forgiveness? Yes___ No___ Explain your response.

_____

_____

_____

_____

_____

_____

_____

_____

SESSION SIX:

COMPLAINING – (PART ONE)

Read Pages: 61-67 of the book entitled "Two Kingdoms."

Only two (2) individuals of the Children of Israel that exited Egypt were allowed to enter the "Promised Land." According to most commentators, there were over two million (2,000,000) individuals that left Egypt. The ratio is a dismal testimony to the group taken out of bondage. Only one (1) person per million (1,000,000) did not murmur or complain and were allowed to reach the "Promised Land."

DEFINITION OF COMPLAINING:

The Biblical expression of dissatisfaction is commonly referred to as "murmuring and complaining."

Complaining may be an expression of pain, dissatisfaction, resentment, unhappiness, discomfort, or discontentment.

Complaining may be expressed through a variety of factors including, but not limited to: demeanor, body language, sarcastic remarks, and behavioral actions.

Complaining is frequently a verbal response to a perceived injustice of a personal wrong or a perceived wrong to another person.

COMPLAINING KEEPS YOU OUT OF
THE "PROMISED LAND:"

Because of the murmuring and complaining of the Children of Israel in the wilderness, only Caleb and Joshua were allowed to enter into the

"Promised Land."

The Children of Israel had seen miracle after miracle and yet murmured (complained) against Moses and Aaron. God protects his appointed leaders. It is a very serious indictment when an individual complains against "God-Appointed" Leaders.

A journey that should have taken forty (40) days became a forty (40) year journey. God, because of their complaining and unbelief, pronounced judgment of one (1) year per day against the Children of Israel. (Numbers 14:34)

Numbers Chapter 14:33-34:

33. And your children shall wander in the wilderness forty years, and bear your whoredoms, until your carcases be wasted in the wilderness. 34. After the number of days in which ye searched the land, even forty days, each day for a year, shall ye bear your iniquities, even forty years, and ye shall know my breach of promise.

Because Caleb and Joshua believed, God allowed them to enter into the "Land of Promise."

Numbers Chapter 14:21-30:

21. But as truly as I live, all the earth shall be filled with the glory of the Lord. 22. Because all those men which have seen my glory, and my miracles, which I did in Egypt and in the wilderness, and have tempted me now these ten times, and have not hearkened to my voice; 23. Surely they shall not see the land which I sware unto their fathers, neither shall any of them that provoked me see it: 24. But my servant Caleb, because he had another spirit with him, and hath followed me fully, him will I bring into the land whereinto he went; and his seed shall possess it. 25. (Now the Amalekites and the Canaanites dwelt in the valley.) To morrow turn you, and get you into the wilderness by the way of the Red sea. 26. And the Lord spake unto Moses and unto Aaron, saying, 27. How long shall I bear with this evil congregation, which murmur against me? I have heard the murmurings of the children of Israel, which they murmur against me. 28. Say unto them, As truly as I live, saith the Lord, as ye have spoken in mine ears, so will I do to you: 29. Your carcases shall fall in this wilderness; and all that were numbers of you, according to your whole number, from twenty years old and upward, which have murmured against me, 30. Doubtless ye shall not come into the land, concerning which I sware to make you dwell therein, save Caleb the son of Jephunneh, and Joshua the son of Nun.

In the New Testament, Paul admonishes individuals not to murmur as some did and were destroyed.

I Corinthians 10:10-11:

10. Neither murmur ye, as some of them also murmured, and were destroyed of the destroyer. 11. Now all these things happened unto them for ensamples: and they are written for our admonition, upon whom the ends of the world are come.

COMPLAINING IS A DISEASE:

Murmuring and complaining is easy to commit. Individuals are not at "ease." The word disease comes from dis and ease. To not be at "ease." Complaining is one of the seven (7) behaviors associated with "External Control Psychology." The other six (6) are criticizing, blaming, nagging, threatening, punishing, and bribing.

I recall a colleague of mine that occasionally used the following phrase. "Vote with your feet." (Get away from complainers and those that have negative influences.)

COMPLAINING FORMULA SIMPLIFIED:

LANE THEORY:

> Complaining = Individual + Dissatisfaction
> Complaining = Individual - Any Want

> *COMPLAINERS SEEM TO HAVE A PREDISPOSITION TO "JUST GIVE UP." HOWEVER, POSSIBLY THEY NEVER INTENDED TO "START."*

Life is full of "ups" and "downs." Individuals do not always get their "way." Complaining may be a way for individuals to keep from admitting the Truth. Complaining is a deterrent to finding Truth. In addition, complaining is a mannerism used for avoidance of admitting personal error and responsibility.

QUESTION:

1. What do you believe are the major dissatisfactions and wants of individuals in our Nation? Briefly describe.

_____

_____

_____

_____

_____

_____

_____

Frequently, verbal complaints are attempts to isolate the problems and make the situation(s) mentally and emotionally manageable. These verbal attacks are attempts to isolate and insulate "self." The individual is not willing to "work-through" the situation, but instead, complains. I refer to it as: "The Lazy-Man's Resolve."

THE LAZY-MAN'S RESOLVE:

These individuals do not want to resolve difficulties; they just want to verbally express their disappointment by complaining. Thus, The Lazy-Man's Resolve. However, these individuals are caught in their own "Web of Self-Deceit."

A productive and successful life requires work. Individuals need to be proactive to resolve their problems. Hunger is a motive to work. "No Work, No eat." Some individuals, because of laziness, become a disgrace to themselves, their family, their society, and God. God declares: "If you don't provide for your family, you are worse than an infidel." I Timothy 5:8: _But if any provide not for his own, and specially for those of his own house, he hath denied the faith, and is worse than an infidel._

If individuals would first pay their obligations (bills) and then eat, their spending behavior(s) would change. Going hungry is a "motivator" for an individual to work.

Indebtedness stifles an individual's present and future financial success. Therefore, always spend less than you earn.

QUESTION:

2. Does the "LAZY MAN'S RESOLVE" seem to explain some difficulties in our Nation? Yes___ No___ Briefly explain.

_____

_____

_____

_____

_____

> ## THE LADDER OF SUCCESS
> ## IS NOT AN ESCALATOR

Complaining causes an individual to place their life on "pause." They are in a "holding pattern." Their life is "on hold" or in a continual "orbit." Complainers are individuals that let "little-things" become the central focus of their conversations.

> ## COMPLAINERS NEED
> ## TO STOP "RECYCLING"
> ## THEIR PROBLEMS

Unfortunately, some complainers do not want a solution. A solution, to their perceived problem, would negate and eliminate a portion of their life. (The portion of their life they spend complaining.)

Complainers hunger for recognition and feel they have the God-given duty and obligation to let the entire world know of their perceived "wrongs."

> ## COMPLAINING IS LIKE SITTING IN A
> ## ROCKING CHAIR, IT GIVES YOU
> ## SOMETHING TO DO, BUT IT DOESN'T
> ## GET YOU ANYWHERE.

Complainers seem to be talkative communicators, but procrastinate in completing the immediate tasks given them. Their incessant "chatter" interferes with their performance. In my College Communication Classes, I used a term for the talkative. I referred to them as: "BIONIC JAWS."

It is difficult when "greeting" a person and you ask them "How Are You?" Then, you hear a ten (10) to fifteen (15) minute "health-history." As you leave you think, "Please let me remember to just say 'Hello' the next time I meet them."

COMPLAINERS WOULD
RATHER TALK
THAN TAKE ACTION.
THUS, THEY PROCRASTINATE!

Some individuals spend their life reminiscing the past, complaining about the present, and fearing the future.

It is difficult for complainers to relax because their emotions are disturbed.

QUESTION:

3. Do you believe the "work-ethic" continues to decline in our Nation? Yes___ No___ Briefly explain.

_____

_____

_____

_____

_____

_____

4. Do you believe Christians should be concerned with the "work-ethic" of others? Yes___ No___ Briefly explain.

_____

_____

_____

_____

_____

_____

_____

5. Do you believe there is anything an individual can do to stop others from complaining? Yes___ No___ Briefly explain.

_____

_____

_____

_____

_____

_____

_____

SESSION SEVEN:

COMPLAINING – (PART TWO)

Read Pages: 67-71 of the book entitled "Two Kingdoms."

LIFE SHOULD BE
ENJOYED,
NOT ENDURED

Show me a chronic complainer and I'll show you a very miserable person to be around.

Complaining to others that can do nothing about resolving the problem is a waste of everyone's time. Both the complainer and listener's time is wasted. <u>Complainers waste their emotional energy and your time.</u>

KILLING TIME
IS NOT MURDER,
IT'S SUICIDE!

OLD MOUNTAIN PROVERB:

Never try to teach a pig to sing.
It wastes your time, and annoys the pig.

TIME IS AN EQUALIZER:

All individuals have the same amount of time. Success or failure, for each individual, is predicated upon their efficient use of time. The wise "redeem" (to use wisely) their time.

TIME IS A
VERY PRECIOUS
COMMODITY

QUESTION:

1. Respond to the following two (2) questions regarding time:

(1) How can individuals use their time more efficiently? Briefly explain.

_____

_____

_____

_____

_____

_____

_____

_____

(2) In our Society and Nation, what are some of the major "time-wasters?" Briefly explain.

_____

_____

_____

_____

_____

_____

_____

THREE QUESTION SELF-ASSESSMENT:

During my College Tenure, for student "shock-therapy," I would ask the following three questions:

1. ARE YOU FUN TO BE WITH?

2. IF OTHERS WERE JUST LIKE YOU, WHAT KIND OF GROUP WOULD EXIST?

3. IF YOUR SPOUSE ACTED LIKE YOU, WOULD YOU BE HAPPILY MARRIED? WHAT KIND OF MARRIAGE WOULD YOU HAVE? (ACTUALLY, WOULD YOU EVEN HAVE A MARRIAGE?)

HONESTLY ASK YOURSELF
THE ABOVE THREE QUESTIONS!

WE ARE BORN WITH OUR
MOUTH OPEN AND OUR
EYES CLOSED. IT IS A
"LIFE LONG" PROCESS
ATTEMPTING TO
REVERSE THE SITUATION!

QUESTION:

2. Do you believe asking the "Three Question Assessment" could change an individual's thinking-pattern? Yes___ No___ Briefly explain.

_____

_____

_____

_____

_____

_____

_____

COMPLAINING CAMOUFLAGES COMPLACENCY:

Complaining may be a way to camouflage complacency. Hidden motives and intent may be the motivation for complaining. Complacency breeds contempt and contempt yields a bad attitude.

ANY "FOOL" CAN CRITICIZE
AND MOST "FOOLS" DO

Yes, complainers are foolish and bring dire emotional injuries upon themselves and those close to them. Family, friends, and co-workers all pay a "price" for being close to a complainer.

COMPLAINING IGNITES AND FUELS THE FIRE OF DISCORD:

Individuals that complain usually have an excessively high view of themselves. In addition, complaining is infectious.

Lucifer, "The Father of Lies," self-destructs and causes one-third (1/3) of the angelic host to lose their heavenly positions. Lucifer was responsible for an original item. (The item of "iniquity.") There was no iniquity, until iniquity was found in him. *Ezekiel 28:15: Thou wast perfect in thy ways from the day that thou wast created, till iniquity was found in thee.*

Again, the Children of Israel murmured and complained and only two (2) individuals escaped the grasp of the complaining. Only Caleb and Joshua were not absorbed in the "deceitful web" of complaining.

HABITUAL COMPLAINERS:

Habitual complainers are consumed by their "life-of-complaining." Those close to a habitual complainer are aware of their rhetoric before they speak. Chronic complainers may be described as highly efficient in expressing dissatisfaction, hungering for attention, and continuously living in outrage. These individuals seem to have adopted the personal philosophy of: "It Pays to Complain" or "IT'S GAIN TO COMPLAIN." Therefore, I believe their life can be summated as a: HABITUAL COMPLAINER.

COMPLAINERS ISOLATE THEMSELVES:

Who likes to be around a "complainer?" Only other "complainers" like to be around "complainers." Other individuals attempt to avoid "complainers."

COMPLAINERS
DESIRE PEER APPROVAL,
BUT
"SELF-DESTRUCT"

Rarely will someone come to assist them. Their continual barrage of complaints drives away those that might be able to assist. The old saying, "I can't complain, nobody listens," is not true. Others do listen and are tired of listening. Thus, the complainer is left alone to fend for themselves. Complainers become isolated on their own toxic island of despair and hopelessness.

The complainer doesn't seem to realize that other individuals are not always empathetic to their complaints.

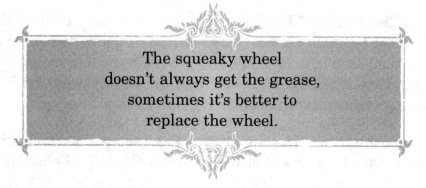

The squeaky wheel
doesn't always get the grease,
sometimes it's better to
replace the wheel.

QUESTION:

3. Have you experienced situations where individuals were replaced because of their continual complaining? Yes___ No___ Briefly explain.

_____

_____

_____

_____

_____

_____

_____

4. Why do you believe it seems so easy to identify the problems (difficulties) of other individuals and not be able to identify our own problems (difficulties)?

_____

_____

_____

_____

_____

_____

_____

5. Have you observed (experienced) the destructive power of criticism in a Church Environment? Yes___ No___ If yes, briefly explain.

_____

_____

_____

_____

_____

_____

_____

SESSION EIGHT:

COMPLAINING – (PART THREE)

Read Pages: 71-75 of the book entitled "Two Kingdoms."

QUICK, HIDE, HERE THEY COME:

It is deemed, by some, necessary to play "hide and seek" with habitual complainers. The "hide-and-seek" principle is: "I will hide, and you try to find me." Avoiding the chronic complainer is for personal emotional survival. Who really wants to listen to repetitive complaints? Answering machines have value to "screen-out" unwanted and unsolicited telephone calls.

Complainers seldom seem to "figure-out" that people are avoiding them. The complainer is so intent on telling their "one-sided" story they fail to recognize they are being avoided. Their view of "self" overrides all other external information, regardless of how apparent and pronounced the communication is delivered. For emotional preservation and personal productivity reasons, it seems imperative to "hide" from some individuals.

QUESTION:

1. Have you been in situations that you had to "hide" from another individual for emotional survival? Yes___ No___

    a. If yes, briefly explain.

_____

_____

_____

_____

_____

b. If no, what do you contribute your success in the avoidance of these situations? Briefly explain.

_____

_____

_____

_____

_____

AVOID CHRONIC COMPLAINERS
COMPLAINING IS CONTAGIOUS

Complaining is infectious and is analogous to a blister or a fly that continuously pesters an individual.

Just as "second-hand" smoke is unhealthy, so is "second-hand" complaining.

DO NOT REPEAT
THE CONVERSATIONS
OF CHRONIC COMPLAINERS:
THEIR WORDS ARE TOXIC.

COMPLAINERS
RECYCLE
GARBAGE!

Complainers tend to get "stuck" in the "oh woe is me" syndrome. Complainers get "stuck" in a situation they cannot solve and become unhappy. Their energy is dissipated by their negative reactions.

NEGATIVE EMOTIONS
THWART AN INDIVIDUAL'S
CREATIVE ABILITIES

Complainers are not able to relax because their emotions remain disturbed. Thus, their inability to relax causes them to "vent" additional complaints. Frequently, complainers do not "vent" to the right person. They consume the time of those that have no authority, or the ability, to make a difference in their situation.

COMPLAINERS MAKE
FUTILE ASSAULTS

Complaining becomes a daily continual effortless habit. Therefore, the complainer has only themselves to blame for their "self-induced" emotional turmoil and personal difficulties.

COMPLAINERS DO NOT
COMPLAIN BECAUSE
THEY HAVE PROBLEMS;

COMPLAINERS
HAVE PROBLEMS
BECAUSE THEY
COMPLAIN.

Complainers are actually asserting their deficiency to resolve their personal difficulties.

COMPLAINTS AND CRITICISMS
VALIDATE AN INDIVIDUAL'S
IGNORANCE AND INEFFICIENCY
IN DEALING WITH
LIFE'S CIRCUMSTANCES

COMPLAINING IS A SELF-INDICTMENT:

Complaining validates an individual's ignorance and inefficiency in dealing with life's circumstances. Complainers do not accept that they may be wrong. An acceptance of their infallibility and propensity to error keeps them externally focused. They proclaim their inefficient abilities to solve life's circumstances. Therefore, habitual complainers never mature. They always see the "trees" and not the "forest."

**FACE YOUR PROBLEMS,
OTHERWISE,
YOU WILL NOT
SEE THEM COMING!**

QUESTION:

2. Complaining, by some individuals, seems to "snowball" (increases with time).

   a. What are some of the reasons complaining increases with time? Briefly explain.

   _____

   _____

   _____

   _____

   _____

   b. How can an individual decrease or even stop complaining? Briefly explain.

   _____

   _____

   _____

   _____

CLIQUES VALIDATE BELIEF SYSTEMS:

For social acceptance, all individuals need validation of "self." According to research, individuals develop their self-concept at a very young age. My Doctoral Research was conducted regarding an individual's Self-Concept. Self-Concept may also be expressed as Self-Worth, Self-Value or Self-Esteem. In studies, these terms are frequently used interchangeably. A skewed view of "self" may be developed by "false" validation from close others. A small group bands together and become mutual validation for their individual belief-system. An extension of this concept is the "gang-mentality."

The "gang-mentality" is: "<u>We are</u> the most important and <u>we will</u> try to prove, to all others, that <u>we are</u> the most important."

Gangs deteriorate to the lowest possible level. Dogs in a pack revert to the behavior of the "meanest" animal in the pack. Gang members deteriorate to the vilest individual in the group. Thus, evil is perpetuated to a level that lone individuals would never commit.

Reasoning and communicating does little to deteriorate bad behavior in evil symbiotic-relationships. Unfortunately, force seems the only immediate and long-term deteriorate to evil behavior.

EVIL ONLY UNDERSTANDS FORCE!

QUESTION:

3. Cliques (strong bonds between individuals) validate belief-systems. Discuss the impact(s) of a clique upon individuals:

   a. Family:

   _____
   _____
   _____
   _____
   _____

   b. Friends:

   _____
   _____
   _____
   _____
   _____

   c. Marriage:

   _____
   _____

_____
_____
_____

    d. Church Community:

_____
_____
_____
_____
_____

    e. Work Environment:

_____
_____
_____
_____
_____

    f. An individual's thought patterns:

_____
_____
_____
_____
_____

4. What do you believe are reasonable and appropriate "triggers" (reasons) to leave the association of:

    a. Family:

_____
_____
_____
_____

    b. Friends:

_____
_____
_____
_____

c. Marriage:

_____

_____

_____

_____

d. Church Community:

_____

_____

_____

_____

e. Work Environment:

_____

_____

_____

_____

SESSION NINE:

COMPLAINING – (PART FOUR)

Read Pages: 75-85 of the book entitled "Two Kingdoms."

THE SPOILED CHILD:

Another analogy is the "spoiled child." Complainers, like the "spoiled child" are looking and expecting the parent to "give-in" to their relentless barrage of complaints.

COMPLAINERS ARE
SEEKING ATTENTION

Complainers are seeking attention. Just as the toddler cries and yells, the complainer is seeking attention. In fact, if they do not get their "way" or are not listened to, the complainer exhibits negative behavior. These negative behaviors include arrogant, haughty, and other childish emotional responses. These emotional responses include, but are not limited to: Ignoring others, not speaking to others, pouting, leaving the presence of others, locking themselves in their room, or any other means of "self-removal" from social activities.

COMPLAINING IS AN ADULT FORM OF A CHILD'S TEMPER TANTRUM

QUESTION:

1. Behaviors are habit forming. When encountering an adult having a "child temper tantrum," what are reasonable and appropriate actions (behaviors) for another individual to take? Briefly explain.

_____

_____

_____

_____

_____

_____

_____

COMPLAINERS LIVE IN A PRISON:

Complainers actually imprison themselves away from others. Consequently, others are unable to have an adult relationship with them. Thus, the childish immature behavior becomes their "persona." Each time a situation is encountered that does not meet their expectation, negative and immature behavior is exhibited. The pattern of "self-talk," for the complainer exclaims:

"It worked last time and I believe it will work this time."

COMPLAINING IS A FORM OF DISOBEDIENCE:

The complainer believes, "after all, I just want the outcome to be <u>my way</u> and you need to understand I will not cooperate until it is <u>my way</u>." In fact, the complainer may even purposely disobey or ignore both verbal and written instructions. What a shame to have a child, or an employee that has never "grown-up." A common method of relating to this disobedient personality is to "ignore" them. Let them "stew" in their own mess until they decide to come out of their room (prison) and meet the world again.

REMOVAL OF ONESELF FROM THE PRESENCE OF BAD BEHAVIOR IS AN ADULT RESPONSE.

COMPLAINERS MAY NOT HAVE MIGRAINES, BUT SOME OF THEM ARE "CARRIERS."

COMPLAINERS ARE NOT TEAM-PLAYERS:

Complainers are not "team-players." Selfish and self-centered, the complainer is counter-productive to a healthy business or social environment.

In Management Courses, I referred to three (3) categories of Employees and Managers. I coined what I referred to as the "Three P's of People."

LANE THEORY:

The "Three P's of People" are:

PARASITES
POACHERS
PRODUCERS

Parasites just "live" in an organization and eventually take much of the "Life" out of the group.

Poachers are not very helpful. Poachers claim other's ideas. They cause dissension and are very counter-productive to a group or organization.

Producers carry their own workload and often assist other individuals with their workloads.

QUESTION:

2. Have you observed or worked with individuals that you can readily place in one of the categories mentioned above? (Parasites, Poachers, and Producers) Yes___ No___ How is the Church Community affected and effected by these individuals? Briefly explain.

a. Parasites:

_____

_____

_____

_____

_____

b. Poachers:

_____

_____

_____

_____

_____

c. Producers:

_____

_____

_____

_____

_____

Complainers assert they are innocent victims and may believe they are martyrs.

COMPLAINERS
LIVE IN A
TOXIC BUBBLE
OF "SELF-PITY"

Complainers look through lenses of "SELF-PERCEPTION." They do not evaluate their present circumstances or the future consequences of their current actions.

COMPLAINERS ARE POOR PLANNERS:

Because complainers are poor planners, they have no clearly defined "self-expectations." If an individual does not have clearly defined and realistic goals, they waste time.

POOR PLANNERS
WASTE TIME

Life is unpredictable. All individuals need "flexible" plans. Objectives and goals generate internal motivation. For a productive life, objectives and goals are required to move in a general direction toward a specific destination. A deterrent to complaining are set "goals" and "plans" for the future. Definitive directional goals increase productivity. Goals do not "work" for an individual, the individual "works" for the goal.

GOALS ENCOURAGE
INDIVIDUALS TO FOCUS TOWARD
A PRE-DETERMINED DIRECTION

If an individual does not know where they are going, how will they know when they get there?

COMPLAINERS IGNORE REALITY:

Complainers make grave attempts to convince themselves and others that the circumstance or present situation is not really "how it is."

COMPLAINERS RARELY
ACCEPT WHAT IS
HAPPENING

Complainers want to change the "view" of others. People need to listen and believe their "view." <u>COMPLAINING ONLY CHANGES ATTITUDES, NOT FACTS!</u>

Again, complainers attempt to remove themselves from reality. The complainer's attitude is: "If you need an explanation of the situation, just ask me." These individuals rarely derive satisfaction from helping others.

Complainers believe they are better than others; yet, frequently, they are bitter people and are not happy with themselves.

They are "self-absorbed" and cannot feel sufficient empathy for the misfortune of others, even "close-others."

COMPLAINERS ARE
"SELF-ABSORBED"
AND DO NOT
SHOW EMPATHY

An unwillingness to accept "how things are" will lead to both disapproval and disdainful contempt for others.

"SELF-ABSORBED" INDIVIDUALS
RARELY HAVE SATISFACTORY
RELATIONSHIPS

Complainers believe nothing is ever good enough for them. No matter what the outcome, they remain unhappy individuals.

Complainers rarely recognize that their constant complaining increases internal emotional turmoil and depression. In fact, <u>complaining is a "trigger" for depression</u>.

MATURATION:

Maturation, by definition, is the ability to differentiate between circumstances and relationships. An individual's ability to isolate behavioral differences is an indication of maturity. Just because an individual is upset with one situation, they should not be upset with other situations. Maturation is the ability to differentiate difficulties and the non-transference of those difficulties to other relationships. Thus, the ability to differentiate between circumstances and relationships is the definition of "maturation." Complaining causes individuals to cease their maturation, emotional stability, and problem-solving abilities. An individual's response to circumstances indicates and reveals their maturation level. Blaming others and complaining is an external focus, not an internal focus. Thus, maturation growth is slow because of excessive external focus. As a result of excessive external focus, individuals do not deal with their own "shortcomings."

EXTERNAL STIMULANTS PAUSE MATURATION:

The "use" of an external stimulant causes a "pause" in an individual's maturation. For some, an external stimulant is frequently used to "cope" with life's circumstances. As conflicts and emotional turmoil increases, individuals look for "relief."

Attempts to obtain "relief" may include, but not limited to: Alcohol, drugs, and addictive behaviors. When stress levels reach the level that causes an individual to "use" an external stimulant, their emotional maturation ceases. Therefore, their "emotional–age" is the beginning of their continual "use" of external stimulants.

Individuals that resolve their difficulties through natural behavioral development, hopefully, become "mature" adults. Individuals that continually resolve their difficulties through an external stimulant, remain "immature" adolescents.

Thus, there are adults attempting to raise children and they, themselves, have only a twelve (12) or thirteen (13) year old "emotional-age." Their young "emotional-age," is because each time they have encountered stress, conflicts, and personal turmoil, they have "used" an external stimulant. Therefore, although attaining an "adult" age, they continue to exhibit "adolescent" behavior(s).

The whole world will have to suffer because I am not getting my way. "In fact, if you do not do what I want to do, you will be sorry. I will pout, cry, whine and continue to complain until I do get my way."

If an individual really wants to change and cease from complaining, it is a simple process, merely <u>stop</u>.

QUESTION:

3. Some individuals seem to never mature. Do you believe there is anything that another individual can do to assist in their maturity? Yes___ No___ Briefly explain.

_____

_____

_____

_____

_____

_____

_____

THE ONLY CURE
FOR BEHAVIORAL CHANGE IS:
<u>STOP THE BEHAVIOR</u>

Some couples have part of their relationship based on mutual complaining. Therefore, a symbiotic communication continues and eventually causes their relationship to stop growing. This occurs because their mutual focus is constantly focused on external situations outside their personal relationship. Ultimately, there are disagreements and both have not learned to accept personal responsibility and thus withdraw for self-preservation. These individuals blame each other for their minor non-reconciled differences. Their "world" is based upon their personal satisfaction and self-focus. They have become emotionally unstable and cannot move beyond the relational differences, even if the differences are minuscule and minor.

COMPLAINERS BECOME
"NIT PICKY" ABOUT
THE SMALLEST ISSUES

COMPLAINING IS A FORM OF GOSSIP:

Complainers tend to "say too much." Because of their habitual "talkative" demeanor, it is difficult for them to remain silent. Their "talkative" complaining frequently reveals the most intimate "secrets" and personal matters of others. There should be a "Complaint Department" at each social gathering for complainers. (A trash can should be placed in the room and marked "Complaint Department.")

REMEMBER,
COMPLAINERS ARE
"TALKERS"

COMPLAINERS ARE BORING:

As part of my lecture series in Human Behavior Classes, I attempted to provoke student thought by stating: "Never tell anyone you are bored." When a person proclaims "I am bored," in my presence, I'm tempted to say: "You're right, you are one of the most 'boring' individuals I have been around." (Of course, I have never said this, but I've been tempted.")

It is not the responsibility of anyone to entertain another individual. Every individual should assume personal responsibility for their emotional health.

COMPLAINERS ARE
POOR PROBLEM-SOLVERS:

Complainers have poor problem-solving skills. They do not "own" the responsibility for their misfortune. Their search is focused upon a pre-determined criterion to blame others. Seldom, if ever, do they look internally for any acceptance of personal blame. Thus, their problem-solving abilities are limited to a myopic view. Complainers have poor abilities to solve their problems because of such a limited focus.

COMPLAINERS
ARE POOR
PROBLEM-SOLVERS

This pattern of poor problem-solving is analogous to addictive behavior. According to their perception, they have only "one-way" to look at all situations. Thus, their problem-solving skills and social development is stunted. It is easy to find fault, but not so easy to find solutions. The complainer is an expert in finding problems, but rarely finds meaningful solutions.

COMPLAINERS
ARE MUCH BETTER
AT FINDING PROBLEMS
THAN FINDING SOLUTIONS

CONCLUSION:

Complaining keeps an individual out of the "Promised Land." Complaining asserts an accusation not only against an individual's personal circumstances, but also against GOD. After all, it is GOD that designs and develops the circumstances that will bring further Spiritual Growth into the lives of His children. If you are a Christian, always remember:

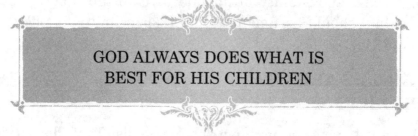

GOD ALWAYS DOES WHAT IS
BEST FOR HIS CHILDREN

Therefore, if you are HIS child, accept what is happening in your life. It is actually "good for your Spiritual development."

4. After your studying the topic regarding "COMPLAINING," what, in your opinion, are the most serious difficulties caused by the Complainer?

_____

_____

_____

_____

_____

_____

_____

_____

SESSION TEN:

THANKSGIVING AND PRAISE

Read Pages: 86-95 of the book entitled "Two Kingdoms."

SACRIFICES THAT MAY BE OFFERED:

1. A sacrifice of righteousness. *Philippians 4:18: But I have all, and abound: I am full, having received of Epaphroditus the things which were sent from you, an odour of a sweet smell, a sacrifice acceptable, well pleasing to God. Psalms 4:5: Offer the sacrifices of righteousness, and put your trust in the Lord.*

2. A broken spirit: a broken and contrite heart. *Psalms 51:17: The sacrifices of God are a broken spirit: a broken and a contrite heart, O God, thou wilt not despise.*

3. A sacrifice of praise and doing good. *Hebrews 13:15-16: 15. By him therefore let us offer the sacrifice of praise to God continually, that is, the fruit of our lips giving thanks to his name. 16. But to do good and to communicate forget not: for with such sacrifices God is well pleased.*

4. A sacrifice of joy and singing. *Psalms 27:6: And now shall mine head be lifted up above mine enemies round about me: therefore will I offer in his tabernacle sacrifices of joy; I will sing, yea, I will sing praises unto the Lord.*

5. A sacrifice of thanksgiving. *Psalms 116:17: I will offer to thee the sacrifice of thanksgiving, and will call upon the name of the Lord.*

6. A sacrifice of praise. *Jeremiah 33:11: The voice of joy, and the voice of gladness, the voice of the bridegroom, and the voice of the bride, the voice of them that shall say, Praise the Lord of hosts: for the Lord is good; for*

his mercy endureth for ever: and of them that shall bring the sacrifice of praise into the house of the Lord. For I will cause to return the captivity of the land, as at the first, saith the Lord.

QUESTION:

1. Praise seems to only come easy when all is "going well." Sacrificial praise is directly proportional to the difficulties encountered at the time the praise is being offered. Are there methods or means that individuals can use to praise the Lord more frequently?
   Yes___ No___ Briefly explain.

_____

_____

_____

_____

_____

ANTIDOTE FOR COMPLAINING:

Praise is the antidote for complaining. Offering praise changes an individual's attitude and life. Seemingly, most individuals want change in their life. Of course, the change needs to be done by someone else. However, the only individual that we can change is ourselves. Changing ourselves gives us control over our environment. In other words, rather than attempting to change others, changing ourselves changes everything around us.

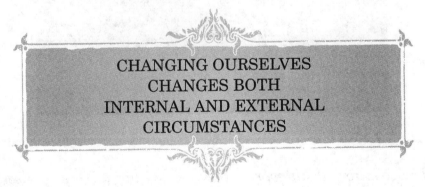

CHANGING OURSELVES
CHANGES BOTH
INTERNAL AND EXTERNAL
CIRCUMSTANCES

PRAYER IS A PRIVILEGE:

Prayer is a privilege. Most of us will never have an opportunity to meet with dignitaries of this World, but we have the privilege to communicate directly with God.

PRAYER AND PRAISE ARE CAUSAL:

Most Christians believe that Prayer changes things. However, as related in James 4:2-3, we are granted those things that will not be consumed on our lusts.

James 4:2-3:

2. Ye lust, and have not: ye kill, and desire to have, and cannot obtain: ye fight and war, yet he have not, because ye ask not. 3. Ye ask, and receive not, because ye ask amiss, that ye may consume it upon your lusts.

Prayer is an awesome responsibility. The granting of some petitions would be destructive for the petitioner.

Psalms 106:13-15:

13. They soon forgat his works; they waited not for his counsel. 14. But lusted exceedingly in the wilderness, and tempted God in the desert. 15. And he gave them their request; but sent leanness into their soul.

Notice the granting of some petitions will send "leanness" into the soul. An individual's soul is to be vibrant and alive. The soul is the emotional center of our life. "Leanness" connotes a deficiency in an individual's "soul-

The Two Kingdoms Study Guide

life." We should always ask the Holy Spirit to censor our petitions to God. In addition, prayer petitions, for personal "wants," should be finalized with "Thy will be done."

The causal relationship between sanctioned prayers and selfish prayers is related to spiritual maturity. Small children frequently ask for many things the parent does not grant.

THANK GOD
THAT SOME
OF OUR PRAYERS
ARE NOT ANSWERED

Prayer should sanction all of our actions. Martin Luther's comment: "I have so much to do today; I had better spend more time in Prayer." Lack of Prayer and Praise causes an individual to have difficulties. We can, by the privilege of Praising God, change circumstances.

I John 5:14-15:

14. And this is the confidence that we have in him, that, if we ask any thing according to his will, he heareth us: 15. And if we know that he hear us, whatsoever we ask, we know that we have the petitions that we desired of him.

The petitions are granted, if we pray <u>according to His will</u>. I believe the petitions, prayed during periods of Praise and Thanksgiving, are birthed by the Holy Spirit.

Caution is advised when praying for circumstances that we desire and are not birthed from God. Of course, God wants only the best for our life and the lives of others.

"Is not faith the precognition of what <u>God wants to do</u>?"

FIND OUT WHAT
GOD WANTS TO DO
AND THEN PRAY

RESULTS OF PRAISE:

Praise unlocks all barred doors. Sometimes, those bound in prison or let down in a dungeon escaped by Praise and Thanksgiving. In Acts 16:25-40, Paul and Silas are delivered from prison by an earthquake.

Acts 16: 25-40:

25. And at midnight Paul and Silas prayed, and sang praises unto God: and the prisoners heard them. 26. And suddenly there was a great earthquake, so that the foundations of the prison were shaken: and immediately all the doors were opened, and every one's bands were loosed. 27. And the keepers of the prison awaking out of his sleep, and seeing the prison doors open, he drew out his sword, and would have killed himself, supposing that the prisoners had been fled. 28. But Paul cried with a loud voice, saying, Do thyself no harm: for we are all here. 29. Then he called for a light, and sprang in, and came trembling, and fell down before Paul and Silas. 30. And brought them out, and said, Sirs, what must I do to be saved? 31. And they said, Believe on the Lord Jesus Christ, and thou shalt be saved, and thy house. 32. And they spake unto him the word of the Lord, and to all that were in his house. 33. And he took them the same hour of the night, and washed their stripes; and was baptized, he and all his, straightway. 34. And when he had brought them into his house, he set meat before them, and rejoiced, believing in God with all his house. 35. And when it was day, the magistrates sent the serjeants, saying, Let those men go. 36. And the keeper of the prison told this saying to Paul, The magistrates have sent to let you go: now therefore depart, and go in peace. 37. But Paul said unto them, They have beaten us openly uncondemned, being Romans, and have cast us into prison; and now do they thrust us out privily? nay verily, but let them come themselves and fetch us out. 38. And the serjeants told these words unto the magistrates: and they feared, when they heard that they were Romans. 39. And they came and besought them, and brought them out, and desired them to depart out of the city. 40. And they went out of the prison, and entered into the house of Lydia: and when they had seen the brethren, they comforted them, and departed.

PRAISE INCREASES ENERGY:

Frequently, Christians experience an increase of energy in the presence of the Holy Spirit. Individuals, sometimes extremely tired, report an increase in energy and a "resting-factor" when attending church services. Praise is "health-food" for an individual's spirit. The Holy Spirit energizes the human spirit and releases energy into the physical body. When we enter into the presence of the Lord, we obtain "soul-food" and experience rest and relaxation.

David's success was related to his Praise and Thanksgiving. He praised and made efforts and proclamations continually to the Lord. He entered the presence of the Lord with gladness and with singing.

Psalms 100:4: Enter into his gates with Thanksgiving, and into His courts with praise: be thankful unto Him, and bless His name.

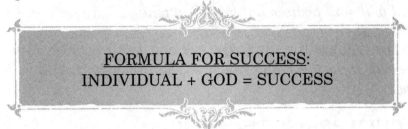

FORMULA FOR SUCCESS:
INDIVIDUAL + GOD = SUCCESS

REASONS TO PRAISE THE LORD:

1. <u>God inhabits the praise of His people</u>. *Psalms 22:3: But thou art holy, O thou that inhabitest the praises of Israel.*

2. <u>God is worthy of Praise</u>. *Psalms 18:3: I will call upon the Lord, who is worthy to be praised: so shall I be saved from mine enemies.*

3. <u>Praise God for His mighty acts</u>. *Psalms 150:2: Praise him for his mighty acts: praise him according to his excellent greatness.*

4. <u>Praise glorifies God</u>. *Psalms 50:23: Whoso offereth praise glorifieth me: and to him that ordereth his conversation aright will I shew the salvation of God.*

5. <u>Praise precedes victory</u>. *II Chronicles 20:21-22: And when he had consulted with the people, he appointed singers unto the Lord, and that should praise the beauty of holiness, as they went out before the army, and to say, Praise the Lord; for his mercy endureth for ever. And when they began to sing and to praise, the Lord set ambushments against the children of Ammon, Moab, and mount Seir, which were come against Judah; and they were smitten.*

WHEN TO PRAISE THE LORD:

1. <u>At all time</u>. *Psalms 34:1: I will bless the Lord at all times: his praise shall continually be in my mouth.*

2. <u>Always give thanks</u>. *Ephesians 5:19-20: Speaking to yourselves in psalms and hymns and spiritual songs, singing and making melody in your heart to the Lord: Giving thanks always for all things unto God and the Father in the name of our Lord Jesus Christ.*

3. <u>When our souls are cast down</u>. *Psalms 42:11: Why are thou cast down, O my soul? And why are thou disquieted within me? Hope thou in God: for I shall yet praise him, who is the health of my countenance, and my God.*

4. <u>As long as we have any being</u>. *Psalms 146:2: While I live will I praise the Lord: I will sing praises unto my God while I have any being.*

5. <u>From the rising of the sun to the evening</u>. *Psalms 113:3: From the rising of the sun unto the going down of the same the Lord's name is to be praised.*

WHO SHOULD PRAISE THE LORD:

1. <u>Everything that has breath</u>. *Psalms 150:6: Let every thing that hath breath praise the Lord. Praise ye the Lord.* This verse is the last verse in the Book of Psalms. David ends his Psalms with the proclamation that: *"every thing that hath breath praise the Lord."*

2. <u>Praise him while you are alive</u>. Praise Him while we are living, because in death, we Praise not the Lord. *Psalms 115:17: The dead praise not the Lord, neither any that go down into silence.*

QUESTION:

2. Both Praise and Prayer for most individuals is cyclical. What, if anything, can be done for individuals to be consistent in Prayer and Praise? Briefly explain.

_____

_____

_____

_____

_____

_____

3. Prayers are petitions to God. These petitions include, but are not limited to:

    a. Ourselves

    b. Our Family

    c. The Salvation of Others

    d. For God to Assist Others

What percentage of time do you believe the average Christian spends in each of these areas?

  e. Ourselves   _____

  f. Our Family   _____

  g. The Salvation of Others   _____

  h. For God to Assist Others   _____

TOTAL 100%

4. Some individuals attempt to tithe their time as well as their money.

  a. What are some of the "pitfalls" for individuals becoming too rigid in their spiritual life? Briefly explain.

_____

_____

_____

_____

_____

  b. Individuals are Spirit, Soul, and Body. What are methods that individuals can utilize to be more natural in Prayer and Praise? (In other words, how can an individual become more integrated in everyday life situations?) Briefly explain.

_____

_____

_____

_____

PRIESTLY OFFERINGS OF SACRIFICES:

In the Old Testament, the <u>Priests of Levi</u> offered sacrifices, in their temple, unto God. In the New Testament, the <u>Priests of Believers</u> offer sacrifices, in their temple, unto God. In the New Testament, Christian Believers have become Kings and Priests. *Revelation 1:6: And hath made us kings and priests unto God and his Father; to him be glory and dominion for ever and ever. Amen. I Peter 2:5: Ye also, as lively stones, are built up a spiritual house, an holy priesthood, to offer up spiritual sacrifices, acceptable to God by Jesus Christ.*

OUR BODY IS THE TEMPLE OF GOD:

I Corinthians 3:16: Know ye not that ye are the temple of God, and that the Spirit of God dwelleth in you?

QUESTION:

5. From: (1) the materials in this Chapter, (2) your personal experience, and (3) your observation(s) of others, what do you believe to be some of the "Higher" sacrifices of Praise and Prayers? Briefly explain.

   a. Prayer:

   _____

   _____

   _____

   _____

   _____

   _____

   b. Praise:

   _____

   _____

   _____

   _____

   _____

   _____

SESSION ELEVEN:

IDOLATRY

Read Pages: 96-108 of the book entitled "Two Kingdoms."

DEFINITION OF IDOLATRY:

The definition(s) of idolatry are: (1) worship of an object as a god; (2) attachment or devotion to something; (3) passionate devotion to an object or person.

DEFINITION OF ADDICTION:

The definition of an addiction is: "a compulsive, obsessive, preoccupation with an object, person, or ideology."

Note that idolatry and addiction are similarly defined, and in some instances are synonymous.

Any aspect of life that impedes or interferes with an individual's personal devotion and worship to God is <u>Idolatry</u>. Addictive behavior is predominant in our Nation. Addictions include, but are not limited to:

1. Alcohol
2. Drugs (prescribed and illegal)
3. Food
4. Chocolate
5. Pepsi or Coca Cola
6. Sports
7. Gambling
8. Television
9. Movies
10. Bodybuilding
11. Idolization of a person

12. Religion
13. Reading
14. Work
15. Hobbies
16. Entertainment
17. Internet
18. Computer games
19. Music
20. Sex (The number one addiction in America.)

Any person, object, ideology, or other aspect of life that consumes our thinking or time and is a priority above God is an <u>Idol</u>. <u>Simply stated, an "idol" is what consumes our thinking and time</u>. Our speech is a result of what we are thinking. (Out of the abundance of the heart the mouth speaks.) *Matthew 12:34: for out of the abundance of the heart the mouth speaketh.* <u>We talk about what we are thinking</u>.

QUESTION:

1. What are other addictions (addictive behaviors) not listed? Please list.

_____

_____

_____

_____

_____

2. Some individuals exercise more "will-power" than others. Do you believe it is possible for individuals to increase their "will-power?"
   Yes ___ No ___ Give the reason(s) for your response.

_____

_____

_____

_____

_____

_____

_____

PRIDE IS THE CAUSE OF IDOLATRY AND SHAME:

Proverbs 11:2: When pride cometh, then cometh shame: but with the lowly (humble) is wisdom. Idolatry is also "self-worship." Lifting ourselves above the worship of God. Pleasing "self," instead of God. Being "SELF-CENTERED," not "CHRIST-CENTERED."

SHAME IS THE BASIS OF ALL ADDICTION:

Eventually, an addiction ensnares and enslaves an individual's will, focus and purpose in life. Frequently, addictive behavior is a "cover-up." In fact, addictive behavior is "shame-based." <u>An addiction is an adult pacifier</u>. An individual develops addictive behavior to soothe or make life tolerable. (An individual, although not sometimes personally aware, will increase their addictive behavior during times of stress.) The first thing Adam and Eve attempted to do, after their disobedience in the Garden of Eden, was to "cover-up." *Genesis 3:7: And the eyes of them both were opened, and they knew that they were naked; and they sewed fig leaves together, and made themselves aprons.*

FEAR IS THE BASIS OF SHAME:

Genesis 3:10: And he (Adam) said, I heard thy voice in the garden, and I was afraid, because I was naked; and I hid myself.

Ultimately, an individual's will and desire is encapsulated by their addictive behavior. An individual may think "I can stop this behavior at any time I want to stop." However, the addictive behavior, over time, increases. A larger and larger "dose" is needed (required) in shorter and shorter intervals. Thus, the individual suffers a loss of self-control. Interestingly, studies indicate that the more intelligent (creative) an individual is the more options (ways) they seem to attempt to resolve their addictive behavior. THE ONLY WAY TO QUIT AN ADDICTION IS TO "<u>STOP</u>" THE BEHAVIOR. <u>No other option seems to be a long-term solution.</u>

QUESTION:

3. Pride, Shame and Fear are correlated to addictive behavior(s).
   Give your personal insights, if any, regarding these correlations?
   (How does Pride, Shame, and Fear relate and fuel each other?)

_____

_____

_____

_____

_____

_____

Individuals spend much of their time in entertainment-related activities rather than life-involvement activities.

We need to be "Active Participants" **in** life rather than "Passive Observers" **of** life.

God created the fuel for man's soul as His Spirit. God's Spirit is the only long-term satisfaction for man. Individuals will never be fulfilled and feel complete until there is a personal realization (revelation) that God is the only "Answer" to their "Cravings."

ZIGGURATS:

Some information regarding "ziggurats" was obtained at http://www.biblehistory.com.

A ziggurat was a temple. Frequently located in the middle of a city. Ziggurats were built by the Ur, Mesopotamia, Babylonian, Egyptian, Mayan, Aztec, and Inca civilizations. The term ziggurat means "mountain of god" or "hill of heaven." A ziggurat was a huge "stepped" structure that was a temple or place for the King, Emperor, Pharaoh, Caesar, or other "high-potentate" to proclaim their office of authority. The "top-position" of the structure belonged to the "highest-leader." Frequently, leaders, by self-proclamation have claimed to be "god-man." Thus mandating "worship" and "obedience" by the people they "rule-over."

The headquarters of a major ministry, in the United States, that failed was built in "ziggurat-form." Can you guess who occupied the highest office in the structure? Yes, the leader that failed and was an embarrassment to himself and many others. Even today, some church leaders demand "obedience" to them and are not servants to the people they are supposed to serve, but "lord-over" the people under their influence. Thus, by action(s) proclaiming to be a man above other men, mandating a false "admiration" (worship) and "obedience" by the people they have "rule-over." This group of "supposed" Spiritual leaders are more concerned about the "feeding" of their ego and their own personal financial gain than "feeding" their "flock." <u>Woe unto this group of leaders</u>.

QUESTION:

4. How does any individual "safe-guard" against:

    a. Taking advantage of others?

_____
_____
_____
_____
_____

    b. Harshly ruling over others?

_____
_____
_____
_____

THE CHRISTIAN LIFE IS SUICIDAL:

"I MUST DIE, THAT HE MAY LIVE." (This is contrary to "Natural Man's" logical thinking.) By "Natural Man," I mean the "Adamic-Nature" all individuals receive as they are born and enter this physical world.

I WILL DO IT MYSELF:

The initial disobedience (sin) by Adam and Eve was a declaration of "self-rule." Man's decision to disobey and maintain control by personal decision-making is a continued process of wanting to "self-rule." In fact, the greatest volume of sales, in major bookstores, is the area of "self-help" materials. The propensity of: "I can resolve my own difficulties," and "I know what I want and know how to obtain what I want," is a continued theme of mankind.

QUESTION:

5. The Christian-Life is suicidal. (I must die that He may live.) Do you believe there are ways (methods) that an individual can do to "speed-up" the "dying-process?"

Yes ___ No ___ Give the reason(s) for your response.

_____

_____

_____

_____

_____

_____

_____

CHRISTIAN-INOCULATION:

Some individuals have never "died-to-self." These individuals just have enough of God to be miserable. (They are not "overcomers" in life.) They seem to be "schizoid-Christians." Living one (1) life inside their family structure and another fake-life for others outside their home. Frequently, these individuals "talk" about Christianity to their children, grandchildren, and others. However, they have not been able to "walk" a consistent Christian-Life. The inconsistent behavior observed by their children, grandchildren, and others is what I refer to as "Christian-Inoculation." The individuals that have had close-relationships have been "falsely" vaccinated with a poor supposed "Christian-exposure." Thus, these individuals of "close-relationship(s)" are exposed to a "double-standard." Therefore, they have "no-use" for the supposed represented "Christian-Life." Their internal and external statements proclaim: "Well, it certainly did not work for my parents or grandparents. They cussed, fussed, yelled, screamed, got very angry and would go to church and put on a false image. I do not want anything to do with the church or Christians."

Some leaders cause as many individuals to leave their church (pastorate) as they have individuals to remain in their congregation. Such a negative "Christian-Inoculation" causes some to never seek Christ. Ask the honest spouse and children if you really want to know the "truth."

QUESTION:

6. How do individuals make sure they do not become a poor example and inaccurately "inoculate" their children, grandchildren, or other close associations? Briefly explain.

_____

_____

_____

_____

_____

_____

THE SPEW CREW:

God wants us to be "hot" or "cold," not "lukewarm." If we are not "hot" or "cold," we will get "SPIT." If we are loved, we will get rebuke and chastisement by Christ and His Holy Spirit. In Revelation 3:14-19, John writes to the Loedicean church (referred to as the "last-day" church): *14. And unto the angel of the church of the Leodiceans write; These things saith the Amen, the faithful and true witness, the beginning of the creation of God; 15. I know thy works, that thou art neither cold nor hot: I would thou wert cold or hot. 16. So then because thou art lukewarm, and neither cold nor hot, I will spue (spew) thee out of my mouth. 17. Because thou sayest, I am rich, and increased with goods, and have need of nothing; and knowest not that thou art wretched, and miserable, and poor, and blind, and naked: 18. I counsel thee to buy of me gold tried in the fire, that thou mayest be rich; and white raiment, that thou mayest be clothed, and that the shame of thy nakedness do not appear; and anoint thine eyes with eye-salve, that thou mayest see. 19. As many as I love, I rebuke and chasten: be zealous therefore, and repent.* We need to accept the correction and discipline of God. By God's discipline and correction, we know we are His children.

Hebrews 12:5-14:

5. And ye have forgotten the exhortation which speaketh unto you as unto children. My son, despise not thou the chastening of the Lord, nor faint when thou art rebuked of him: 6. For whom the Lord loveth he chasteneth, and scourgeth every son whom he receiveth. 7. If ye endure chastening, God dealeth with you as with sons; for what son is he whom the father chasteneth not? 8. But if ye be without chastisement, whereof all are partakers, then are ye bastards, and not sons. 9. Furthermore we have had fathers of our flesh which corrected us, and we gave them reverence; shall we not much rather be in subjection unto the Father of spirits, and life? 10. For they verily for a few days chastened us after their own pleasure; but he for our profit, that we might be partakers of his holiness. 11. Now no chastening for the present seemeth to be joyous, but grievous; nevertheless afterward it yieldeth the peaceable fruit or righteousness until them which are exercised thereby. 12. Wherefore lift up the hands which hang down, and the feeble knees; 13. And make straight paths for your feet, lest that which is lame he turned out of the way; but let it rather be healed. 14. Follow peace with all men, and holiness, without which no man shall see the Lord.

THE ANOINTING:

Esther, prior to standing before the King, completed a year-long process of self-purification. Ointments, oils, and soaps were used by her to become "acceptable" to the King. (Esther 2:12-16) This is analogous to the "anointing" process by the Holy Spirit.

The "Fruits" of the Holy Spirit and the "Gifts" of the Holy Spirit exudes a "sweet-smell." The "anointing," of the Holy Spirit, covers the "stink" of our "flesh." The "anointing" is for our approach to the King (King Jesus). Even though others are aware and sense the "sweet-smell," the "anointing" is only for the King. The fragrance from an "anointed" person should create a desire, within other individuals, to prepare for the King.

It appears most individuals cannot handle much of the "anointing." Unless an individual recognizes the "anointing" is an external "gifting" because of a humbled and contrite spirit, the "anointing" soon dissipates. The "anointing" is meant to "please" the King. Receiving any "honor" as though the "anointing" is a "self-induced" quality perverts and prevents the intended use by the Holy Spirit. Thus, for most individuals, the moments of "anointing" are short-lived. Remember, the "anointing" is only intended for preparation to be in the King's presence.

ONLY DEAD MEN SEE GOD:

Moses, in conversation with God, asked to see His (God's) Glory. God responded that no man could see His face and live. However, God showed Moses special favor and allowed His (God's) entire goodness to pass before him (Moses).

Exodus 33:17-20:

17. And the Lord said unto Moses, I will do this thing also that thou hast spoken: for thou hast found grace in my sight, and I know thee by name. 18. And he said, I beseech thee, shew me thy glory. 19. And he said, I will make all my goodness pass before thee, and I will proclaim the name of the Lord before thee; and will be gracious to whom I will be gracious, and will shew mercy on whom I will shew mercy. 20. And he said, Thou canst not see my face: for there shall no man see me and live.

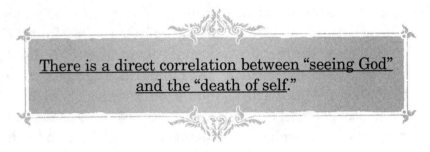

There is a direct correlation between "seeing God" and the "death of self."

The more an individual "receives" from God, the less they "retain" of themselves. The closer an individual "walks with God," their identity is merged with God. ("Not <u>my will</u>, but <u>your will</u> be done.")

In Philippians, Paul gives a brief explanation of his thoughts regarding his physical death. *Philippians 1:21: For to me to live is Christ, and to die is gain.* In Romans, Chapter 12, Paul indicates that it is "reasonable" that those of the "Kingdom of God" present themselves as a "living sacrifice."

Romans 12:1-3:

1. I beseech you therefore, brethren, by the mercies of God, that ye present your bodies a living sacrifice, holy, acceptable unto God, which is your reasonable service. 2. And be not conformed to this world: but be transformed by the renewing of your mind, that ye may prove what is that good, and acceptable, and perfect, will of God. 3. For I say, through the grace given unto me, to every man that is among you, not to think of himself more highly than he ought to think; but to think soberly, according as God hath dealt to every man the measure of faith.

An acceptable offering, by the High Priests of the Old Testament, was "dead flesh." The offering was given to God upon an Altar, in the <u>Outer Court of the Tabernacle</u>, prior to their entering into the <u>Holy Place</u>. <u>If you want to enter into a Holy Place with God, offer a sacrifice of "dead flesh" upon the altar of your heart</u>. (An offering was always prepared by the Priest(s) before entering into the Holy Place.)

DEAD MAN WALKING:

The phrase "Dead Man Walking" is spoken as a convicted prisoner is escorted to the death chamber. It is spoken so that others, if they desire, may be respectful and reverent during the last minutes of the "soon to die" convict's life.

Hopefully, as Christians mature, there is a respect and reverence for others that have attained an "anointing" of God. The "anointing" and presence of God is only attained by personal "death of self." Individuals that have begun the "Death-Walk," realize the anguish and agony of attaining and continuing the "Death-Walk." There should be a respect and reverence for those on the "Death-Walk." Paul states they are worthy of "double honor." (Not the honoring of themselves, by themselves, but respect from others.) Honor should not be a "self-proclamation." Even Jesus would not "honor" himself. In *John 8:54, Jesus answered, "If I honour myself, my honour is nothing: it is my Father that honoureth me; of whom ye say, that he is your God."* Do not look to receive honor from men. We should only want to please God.

If individuals begin "honoring" each other, it will affect their <u>faith</u> in God. *John 5:44. How can ye believe, which receive honour one of another, and seek not the honour that cometh from God only?* Do not give gloating "honor" to each other. <u>An individual's value is directly proportional to the amount of "God's Presence" contained in their "vessel."</u> (Nothing else is of value to God or others.)

Possibly you, reading this book, will become a "great vessel" of God that carries the "Presence of God." God is looking for individuals to reveal His strength to the whole earth. *II Chronicles 16:9. For the eyes of the Lord run to and from throughout the whole earth, to shew himself strong in the behalf of them whose heart is perfect toward him.* <u>God is constantly searching to reveal Himself strong in the life of those whose heart is perfect toward Him.</u>

QUESTION:

7. Have you seen Christian examples that each time you are in their presence, they motivate you to become closer to the King (King Jesus)? Yes ___ No __ If yes, describe these individuals.

_____

_____

_____

8. How can an individual receive a greater "anointing" of God? Briefly explain.

MOSSAI TRIBE:

Reverend Ralph Mahoney, Founder and President of World MAP, related in a sermon information regarding the Mossai Tribe of Africa. I was privileged to serve as a Board Member of World MAP for over twenty (20) years.

<u>Wealth Accumulation</u>: The Mossai Tribe of Africa is an interesting study. They believe that God gave their tribe all the cattle on the Earth. If you have a cow, it is theirs and they go out quite regularly to reclaim their property. Thus, they are not very popular with their neighboring tribes.

They build their homes and streets with cow dung. The women place wet dung in their hair for decorative and beautification purposes. Each member of the village spends great amounts of time accumulating dung for personal use. In addition, they stockpile all the dung they can collect in their villages. Their individual Village Chieftain's wealth is measured by the size of the village "dung-hill." When the Chieftain dies, they burrow back in the "dung-hill" and lay their Chieftain to rest, and recover him with the dung. There he lays, in all the wealth he has attained. A witness and testament to others of the wealth he had been able to accumulate during his lifetime. <u>The "dung-heap" is a monument to the Chieftain's "life-achievements" and "personal-glory."</u>

Some individuals, in Western Cultures, have other collections. These collections may include: A Lexus, BMW or Mercedes, more and better furniture, clothing, jewelry, a truck, a larger home, a vacation home, a motorhome, a boat, etc. Frequently, individuals desire to impress others with their "Things." Showing, as many others as possible, that <u>they</u> have the <u>bigger and better</u> "heap."

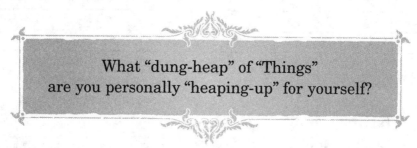

What "dung-heap" of "Things"
are you personally "heaping-up" for yourself?

QUESTION:

9. In our society (Nation), how can individuals become less materialistic? Briefly explain.

_____

_____

_____

_____

_____

_____

10. What, if anything, can individuals do to influence the behavior of others to become less materialistic? Briefly explain.

_____

_____

_____

_____

_____

_____

_____

SESSION TWELVE:

PORNOGRAPHY

Read Pages: 109-113 of the book entitled "Two Kingdoms."

ATTENTION VOYEURS AND PEEPING TOMS:

Pornography is direct from the "pits" of Hell. Pornography will destroy your mind (soul-life). Pornography, like some drugs, can become instantaneously addictive.

A dear friend and colleague, Dean of Health Sciences, prepared for a second career prior to his retirement from the College. He had a humble spirit. He had studied for the priesthood in the early years of his life. He was "well-read" and I enjoyed many lengthy conversations with him during our tenure at the College.

Prior to his retirement, he completed his Marriage Family and Child Counseling (MFCC) Credential. He shared, with me, startling statistics regarding the pronounced extent of pornographic behavior in our Nation. At that time, over sixty-percent (60%) of our Nation's male population was addicted to pornography of some form. Another alarming fact, for me, was that there was no difference in those who professed themselves to be "Christians" and "non-Christians." Christian Leaders, Ministers, and seemingly stalwart members of a church were not immune from this evil travesty. (In other words, over sixty-percent (60%) of these, supposed Christian, individuals were also involved in some form of pornography.)

Pornography is a cancerous disease of the mind and "eats" away an individual's joyful emotional responses. Pornographic behavior causes immense depression and alienation from life (social contacts). (<u>A STEEP SLIPPERY SLOPE OF SEXUAL PERVERSIONS</u>.)

The innocence of children violated by demonic individuals and others taking pleasure in such behavior. Child molesters seem to be in a special abominable category. They are perpetrators of heinous acts, deserving of Eternal Banishment. (<u>SUCH VILE AND INSIDIOUS VIOLATIONS IMPOSED BY CORRUPTED AND EVIL INDIVIDUALS</u>.)

QUESTION:

1. Pornographic materials "injure" and eventually "kill" an individual's "soul-life." What problems occur because of Pornography? Describe and explain.

_____

_____

_____

_____

_____

_____

2. If an individual is involved in Pornographic Behavior(s), how can they stop? Briefly explain.

_____

_____

_____

_____

_____

_____

WORSHIP OF BAAL

Pornographic and elicit behavior was a major part of "Baal-Worship." Baal-Worship was: lewd, lustful, and lascivious.

The three (3) strongest drives in mankind are referred to as the three (3) S's. These three (3) drives are:

1. SOCIAL
2. SEXUAL
3. SPIRITUAL

Baal-Worship incorporated all three (3) of these strong drives. There were major orgies hoping to entice Baal to cohabit with the "goddess" of their agricultural territories. Therefore, the more frequently an individual had sexual-relations it was perceived as additional worship. The worship of Baal was a Social (civil)-duty performed; it was a Sexual-duty performed; and it was a Spiritual-duty performed. Thus, God stated to eliminate all those associated with this worship. It had totally engulfed the people. In fact, God states for the Children of Israel <u>not to do certain acts</u> that had occurred previously because it "pollutes" the land.

Leviticus 18:22-30:

21. Thou shalt not lie with mankind, as with womankind: it is abomination. 23. Neither shalt thou lie with any beast to defile thyself therewith: neither shall any woman stand before a beast to lie down thereto: it is confusion. 24. Defile not ye yourselves in any of these things: for in all these the nations are defiled which I cast out before you: 25. And the land is defiled: therefore I do visit the iniquity thereof upon it, and the land itself vomiteth out her inhabitants. 26. Ye shall therefore keep my statutes and my judgements, and shall not commit any of these abominations; neither any of your nation, nor any stranger that sojourneth among you: 27. (For all these abominations have the men of the land done, which were before you, and the land is defiled:) 28. That the land spue not you out also, when ye defile it, as it spued out the nations that were before you. 29. For whosoever shall commit any of these abominations, even the souls that commit them shall be cut off from among their people. 30. Therefore shall ye keep mine ordinance, that ye commit not any of these abominable customs, which are committed before you, and that ye defile not yourselves therein: I am the Lord your God.

There are various types of sins <u>and all sins are not equal</u>. A "white-lie," so to speak, is not equal to a sin that is an "abomination." God places the sins mentioned in the scriptures above (Leviticus 18:22-30) in a category above the other sins. Defilement is not only of the individuals involved, but there is defilement of the land.

Our nation is polluted by similar abominations of lewd, lustful, and lascivious behaviors. Segments of our nation have adopted some of these behaviors and continue to expand and increase behavioral similarities to Baal-Worship.

QUESTION:

3. Comment regarding the seriousness and consequences of different-type sin(s)? Briefly explain.

_____

_____

_____

_____

_____

_____

SATAN AND HIS WEB

Satan has prepared his attractive "web." Individuals that come near this luring "web" will eventually be snared and trapped. Their "normality" of thinking and reasoning will be eventually destroyed. Their mind becomes a cesspool of debauchery, perversions, and evils of all types.

A recent report indicated that over seventy-percent (70%) of the revenue on the "World Wide Web" is derived from pornographic sites. (What a horrible indictment against our Nation.)

The "stink" ascends up to the Heavens. (This putrid and vile trafficking, occurring twenty-four (24) hours per day, is polluting the entire World.) When will God's "Cup" be full and Judgment is pronounced upon our Nation?

In fact, are we now seeing parts of God's Judgment through some of the Political Decisions and Leadership of our Nation?

IF YOU ARE INVOLVED IN ANY FORM OF PORNOGRAPHIC BEHAVIOR, STOP! "CRY-OUT" TO GOD FOR HIS DELIVERANCE. ASK FOR HIS FORGIVENESS AND CLEANSING. HE CAN AND WILL "SET YOU FREE" AND HEAL YOUR MIND, IF YOU SINCERELY REPENT.

After your sincere repentance, keep yourself clean from this source of vile perverse putrid behavior. "Run Away!" Do Not "Walk Away."

QUESTION:

4. What are the criteria (rules and restrictions) you apply to Movies and Television Programs? What do you believe to be pornographic behavior(s) that are included in Movies and Television Programs? Briefly explain.

_____

_____

_____

a. Which movies and television programs do you allow yourself to view?

_____

_____

_____

_____

b. Which movies and television programs do you allow your children or grandchildren to view?

_____

_____

_____

_____

c. Do you believe some individuals "sneak" and view Movies or Television Programs they are ashamed to tell others they watch? Yes ___ No ___ Briefly explain.

_____

_____

_____

_____

_____

5. Do you believe there are options available for individuals to combat the continued avalanche of Pornographic materials? Yes ___ No ___ Briefly explain.

_____

_____

_____

_____

_____

SESSION THIRTEEN:

HUMILITY

Read Pages: 114-126 of the book entitled "Two Kingdoms."

HUMILITY:

1. Humility is <u>Acceptance</u> of present circumstances and situations. It is not self-brainwashing or the non-recognition of present conditions. Humility accepts where God places us. *Philippians 4:11: for I have learned, in whatsoever state I am, therewith to be content.* WE ARE ENLARGED DURING TIMES OF DISTRESS. *Psalms 4:1: Hear me when I call, O God of my righteousness: thou hast enlarged me when I was in distress; have mercy upon me, and hear my prayer.* In addition, we have the assurance that God hears our Prayers. *Psalms 4:3: But know that the Lord hath set apart him that is Godly for himself, the Lord will hear when I call unto him.*

2. Humility is <u>Submission to Truth</u>. What is Truth? Truth is "How It Is," not how we think it is or how we thought it was going to be. Truth is "HOW IT IS." Our perception is not Truth! THY WORD IS TRUTH. *John 17:14-26: 14. I have given them thy word; and the world hath hated them, because they are not of the world, even as I am not of the world. 15. I pray not that thou shouldest take them out of the world, but that thou shouldest keep them from the evil. 16. They are not of the world, even as I am not of the world. 17. Sanctify them through thy truth: thy word is truth. 18. As thou hast sent me into the world, even so have I also sent them into the world. 19. And for their sakes, I sanctify myself, that they also might be sanctified through the truth. 20. Neither pray I for these alone, but for them also which shall believe on me through their word; 21. That they all may be one; as thou, Father, art in me, and I in thee, that they also may be one in us: that the world may believe that thou hast sent me. 22. And the glory which thou gavest me*

I have given them; that they may be one, even as we are one: 23. I in them, and thou in me, that they may be made perfect in one; and that the world may know that thou hast sent me, and hast loved them, as thou hast loved me. 24. Father, I will that they also, whom thou hast given me, be with me where I am; that they may behold my glory which thou hast given me before the foundation of the world. 25. O righteous Father, the world hath not known thee: but I have known thee, and these have known that thou hast sent me. 26. and I have declared unto them thy name, and will declare it: that the love wherewith thou hast loved me may be in them, and I in them.

3. Humility is <u>Yielding to Authority</u>. Humility is the antithesis of rebellion. *Matthew 11:28-30: 28. Come unto me all ye that labour and are heavy laden, and I will give you rest. 29. Take my yoke upon you, and learn of me; for I am meek and lowly in heart; and ye shall find rest unto your souls. 30. For my yoke is easy, and my burden is light.*

4. Humility is <u>Obedience</u>. Obedience is better than Sacrifice. Just because we go to church and do all that we think or are told to do is not "humbling" ourselves before the Lord. *I Samuel 15:22-23: 22. And Samuel said, Hath the Lord as great delight in burnt offerings and sacrifices, as in obeying the voice of the Lord? Behold, to obey is better than sacrifice, and to hearken than the fat of rams. 23. For rebellion is as the sin of witchcraft, and stubbornness is as iniquity and idolatry. Because thou hast rejected the word of the Lord, he hath also rejected thee from being King.* There is a false perception, by some individuals, thinking they can do something for God. God has told us how much we can do. (NOTHING – ZERO) *John 15:5: I am the vine, ye are the branches: He that abideth in me, and I in him, the same bringeth forth much fruit: for without me ye can do nothing.* Sometimes, individuals are told they need to turn to Jesus because they could do so much for God. Remember, we are only of value to God in the areas we have released to Him. (<u>The areas that we have crucified and died to "self."</u>) Only the work that is birthed by the Spirit of God will last and be beneficial in the Kingdom of God. A listening and obedience to God. The balance between "submission" to God and "service" to God. God working through us.

5. Humility is <u>Servitude</u>. The ability to see the needs of others and gently attempt to meet their need(s). *Mark 10:42-44: 42. But Jesus called them to him, and saith unto them, Ye know that they which are accounted to rule over the Gentiles exercise lordship over them; and their great ones exercise authority upon them. 43. But so shall it not be among you: but*

whosoever will be great among you, shall be your minister. 44. And whosoever of you will be the chiefest, shall be servant of all. THE WAY UP IS DOWN. *Matthew 23:12: And whosoever shall exalt himself shall be abased; and he that shall humble himself shall be exalted.*

6. Humility is <u>Other-Consciousness</u>. (Consciousness of others; prioritizing and placing their needs before our own needs.) The opposite of "self-consciousness." Preoccupation with self is a path of "self-destruction." *Mark 12:28-34: 28. And one of the scribes came, and having heard them reasoning together, and perceiving that he had answered them well asked him, Which is the first commandment of all? 29. And Jesus answered him, The first of all the commandments is, Hear, O Israel; The Lord our God is one Lord: 30. And thou shalt love the Lord thy God with all thy heart, and with all thy soul, and with all thy mind, and with all thy strength: this is the first commandment. 31. And the second is like, namely this, Thou shalt love thy neighbor as thyself. There is none other commandment greater than these. 32. And the scribe said unto him, Well, Master, thou hast said the truth: for there is one God; and there is none other but he: 33. And to love him with all the heart, and with all the understanding, and with all the soul, and with all the strength, and to love his neighbour as himself, is more than all whole burnt offerings and sacrifices. 34. And when Jesus saw that he answered discreetly, he said unto him, Thou are not far from the kingdom of God. And no man after that durst ask him any question.*

7. Humility is <u>Trust</u>. *Proverbs 3:5-6: 5. Trust in the Lord with all thine heart; and lean not unto thine own understanding. 6. In all thy ways acknowledge him, and he shall direct thy paths.*

8. Humility is <u>Patient</u>. Meekness and humility requires an active participation by us. It is not a gift, it is gained by our continual efforts of "dying to self." *James 4:6-10: 6. But he giveth more grace. Wherefore he saith, God resisteth the proud, but giveth grace unto the humble. 7. Submit yourselves therefore to God. Resist the devil, and he will flee from you. 8. Draw nigh to God, and he will draw nigh to you. Cleanse your hands, ye sinners; and purify your hearts, ye double minded. 9. Be afflicted, and mourn, and weep: let your laughter be turned to mourning, and your joy to heaviness. 10. Humble yourselves in the sight of the Lord, and he shall lift you up. I Peter 5:5-7: 5. Likewise, ye younger, submit yourselves unto the elder. Yea, all of you be subject one to another, and be clothed with humility: for God resisteth the proud, and giveth grace to the humble. 6. Humble yourselves therefore under*

the mighty hand of God, that he may exalt you in due time. 7. Casting all your care upon him; for he careth for you.

HUMILITY IS THE ANTHESIS OF PRIDE

QUESTION:

1. Briefly describe what you believe to be the difficulties with fulfilling each area associated with humility. Humility is:

   a. Acceptance:

   _____
   _____
   _____
   _____

   b. Submission to Truth:

   _____
   _____
   _____
   _____

   c. Yielding to Authority:

   _____
   _____
   _____
   _____

   d. Obedience:

   _____
   _____
   _____
   _____

   e. Servitude:

   _____
   _____
   _____
   _____

f. Other-Consciousness:

_____

_____

_____

g. Trust:

_____

_____

_____

h. Patient:

_____

_____

_____

2. If an individual desires to "humble" themselves, are there things they can do? Yes ___ No ___ Briefly explain.

_____

_____

_____

_____

_____

THE KEEPING OF GOD'S LAW BRINGS HIS PROMISES:

Proverbs chapter 3:

1. My son, forget not my law; but let thine heart keep my commandments: 2. For length of days, and long life, and peace, shall they add to thee. 3. Let not mercy and truth forsake thee: bind them about thy neck; write them upon the table of thine heart: 4. So shalt thou find favour and good understanding in the sight of God and man. 5. Trust in the Lord with all thine heart; and lean not unto thine own understanding, 6 In all thy ways acknowledge him, and he shall direct thy paths. 7. Be not wise in thine own eyes: fear the Lord, and depart from evil. 8. It shall be health to thy navel, and marrow to thy bones. 9. Honour the Lord with thy substance, and with the first-fruits of all thine increase: 10. So shall thy barns be filled with plenty, and thy presses shall burst out with new wine. 11. My son, despise not the chastening of the Lord; neither be weary of his correction: 12. For whom the Lord loveth he correcteth; even as a father the son in whom he delighteth. (<u>Obedience and Trust in the Lord leads to Wisdom and Happiness.</u>) *13. Happy is the man that findeth wisdom, and the man that getteth understanding. 14. For the merchandise of it is better than the merchandise of silver, and the gain thereof than fine gold. 15. She is more precious than rubies: and all the things thou canst desire are not to be compared unto her. 16. Length of days is in her right hand; and in her left hand riches and honour. 17. Her ways are ways of pleasantness, and all her paths are peace. 18. She is a tree of life to them that lay hold upon her: and happy is every one that retaineth her.* (<u>Apparently you can have wisdom and understanding and then lose or forsake them.</u>) *19. The Lord by wisdom hath founded the earth; by understanding hath he established the heavens. 20. By his knowledge the depths are broken up, and the clouds drop down the dew. 21. My son, let not them depart from thine eyes: keep sound wisdom and discretion: 22. So shall they be life unto thy soul, and grace to thy neck. 23. Then shalt thou walk in thy way safely, and thy foot shall not stumble. 24. When thou liest down, thou shalt not be afraid: yea, thou shalt lie down, and thy sleep shall be sweet. 25. Be not afraid of sudden fear, neither of the desolation of the wicked, when it cometh. 26. For the Lord shall be thy confidence, and shall keep thy foot from being taken. 27. Withhold not good from them to whom it is due, when it is in the power of thine hand to do it.* (<u>Personal responsibility, not preoccupied with what other people should do.</u>) *28. Say not unto thy neighbor, Go, and come again, and to morrow I will give; when thou hast it by thee. 29. Devise not evil against thy neighbour, seeing he dwelleth securely by thee. 30. Strive not with a man without cause, if he have done thee no harm. 31. Envy thou not the oppressor, and choose none of his ways. 32. For the froward* (<u>purposely stubborn, contrary, adverse; not easily controlled</u>) *is abomination to the Lord: but his secret is with the righteous. 33. The curse of the Lord is in the house of the wicked: but he blesseth the habitation of the just. 34. Surely he scorneth the scorners: but he giveth grace unto the lowly. 35. The wise shall inherit glory: but shame shall be the promotion of fools.*

GOD EXALTS THE HUMBLE:

Humble yourself and God will ultimately exalt you. (Whether in this life or in eternity.) However, attempt to exalt yourself and you will be abased. (Abased means "put-down.")

Some, in "Ministry-Leadership Positions," are only feeding their personal "ego." Jesus said to "feed" my lambs and sheep, not "bleed" my sheep. It is a sad proclamation, that many proclaiming to be "shepherds" are really "hirelings." It is the money and personal attention that are their major motive(s).

Jesus is "building" His Church. You <u>may</u> or <u>may not</u> be a part of His Church. What about your local leader? Have you placed yourself under a "shepherd" or a "hireling." Does your leader have an attitude of a "servant" or are they building their "personal-domain?" Are they "feeding" or "bleeding" the people? Sheep are not too smart, they will follow any "goat" to the slaughter-house. (Frequently, a goat is used to lead sheep, up a ramp, to the slaughter-house.)

QUESTION:

3. If close others, including spiritual-leaders, are not humbling themselves; what are an individual's reasonable and appropriate options? Briefly explain.

_____

_____

_____

_____

_____

4. If an individual remains in an unhealthy spiritual-leadership situation, do they still have options? Briefly explain.

_____

_____

_____

_____

5. If an individual remains in an unhealthy spiritual-leadership situation and begins to complain, what option(s) would you recommend to the individual? Briefly explain.

_____

_____

_____

_____

_____

RIGHT KIND OF ATTITUDE:

Luke 14:7-11: 7. And he put forth a parable to those which were bidden, when he marked how they chose out the chief rooms; saying unto them. 8. When thou art bidden of any man to a wedding, sit not down in the highest room lest a more honourable man than thou be bidden of him; 9. And he that bade thee and him come and say to thee, Give this man place; and thou begin with shame to take the lowest room. 10. But when thou art bidden, go and sit down in the lowest room; that when he that bade thee cometh, he may say unto thee, Friend, go up higher: then shalt thou have worship in the presence of them that sit at meat with thee. 11. For whosoever exalteth himself shall be abased; and he that humbleth himself shall be exalted.

Luke 18:10-14: 10. Two men went up into the temple to pray; the one a Pharisee, and the other a publican. 11. The Pharisee stood and prayed thus with himself, God, I thank thee, that I am not as other men are, extortioners, unjust, adulterers, or even as this publican. 12. I fast twice in the week, I give tithes of all that I possess. 13. And the publican, standing afar off, would not lift up so much as his eyes unto heaven, but smote upon his breast, saying, God, be merciful to me a sinner. 14. I tell you, this man went down to his house justified rather than the other: for every one that exalteth himself shall be abased; and he that humbleth himself shall be exalted.

QUESTION:

6. Maintaining a "good" attitude is an important attribute for Spiritual Maturity. What are some of the "key-factors" for maintaining a "good" attitude? Briefly explain.

_____
_____
_____
_____
_____
_____

ENDING SECTION OF BOOK

NOW IS THE TIME OF SALVATION, THIS OPPORTUNITY MAY NOT COME AGAIN DURING YOUR LIFETIME. <u>Now is the time to make things "right" with God</u>. IF YOU WANT TO BECOME A PART OF THE KINGDOM OF GOD, <u>NOW</u> IS THE TIME!

THIS IS ETERNALLY IMPORTANT FOR YOU! Because of the Eternal Importance to you, I repeat segments printed earlier in this book.

If you are not for certain, that you have accepted JESUS CHRIST into your life; now is the time to accept Him. STOP WHAT YOU ARE DOING AND GET PRIVACY IF YOU CAN. Speak these words, audibly (out loud) in "Faith" believing:

SALVATION PRAYER
JESUS, I ask your forgiveness of all my sins.
I am sorry for all the hurts I have caused,
both to myself and to others.
I truly want you to change my life.
I want to give myself completely to you.
May I know the Peace and Joy
that only you can give.
I want to be an example to
those around me of
how you can change a life.

If you prayed this Prayer, Congratulations! You have taken the first step in becoming what God intended you to be during this earthly life.

In addition, if you are "non-committed" in your "Christian-Life," you need to become determined and focused upon Jesus. Allowing Jesus to live His life through you is the "Christian-Life." Do not confuse living a "good-life" and "giving" your life to Jesus.

Individuals with "good-intentions" are not automatically members of the Kingdom of God. Repent of all your sins and allow Jesus complete access of your life.

If you have not been living a "clean" and "pure" life, you need to make changes in your life. Now is the time to change. STOP WHAT YOU ARE DOING AND GET PRIVACY IF YOU CAN. Speak these words, audibly (out loud) in "Faith" believing:

REDEDICATION PRAYER
Renewed Commitment
JESUS, I ask your forgiveness of all my sins,
I want to rededicate my life to you.
I am sorry for all the hurts I have caused,
to myself and to others.
I truly want you to change my life.
I want to give myself completely to you.
May I know the Peace and Joy
that only you can give.
I want to be an example to
those around me of
how you can change a life.
I rededicate my life and will serve
you with all of my heart.

"Good-intentions" do not guarantee a continued "placement" in the Kingdom of God. Determine to remain "focused" and "committed" for the rest of your life.

If you prayed the prayer of forgiveness or the prayer of "renewed commitment, I would like to hear from you. If you received Jesus into your life or were encouraged by this book, please let me know at the following address:

Dr. Keith Lane
KINGDOM OF GOD TEACHING MINISTRIES
PO BOX 797
Kingsburg, CA 93631-0797
keithlane39@yahoo.com

MY PERSONAL PRAYER TO ALL WHO RECEIVE AND READ THIS BOOK IS: YOU ALLOW GOD CONTINUED ENTRANCE IN YOUR LIFE AND THAT HE WILL BLESS YOU AND KEEP YOU IN HIS CARE.

RECEIVE HIS GRACE AND FORGIVENESS.

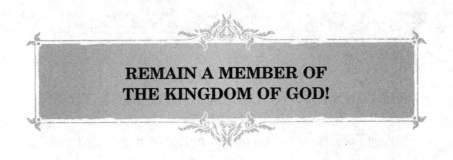

REMAIN A MEMBER OF THE KINGDOM OF GOD!

EXPLANATION OF:
KINGDOM OF GOD TEACHING MINISTRIES
(KOGTM)

KOGTM is a non-profit charitable organization established by me, (Dr. Keith Lane), to fund the printing and distribution of the book and the Study Guide for "The Two Kingdoms."

ALL FUNDS RECEIVED ARE USED TO PRINT AND DISTRIBUTE ADDITIONAL COPIES OF THE BOOK AND STUDY GUIDE FOR:

THE TWO KINGDOMS

Dr. Keith Lane, President
Kingdom of God Teaching Ministries

NOTES:

_____
_____
_____
_____
_____
_____
_____
_____
_____
_____
_____
_____
_____
_____
_____
_____

NOTES:

NOTES:

NOTES:

NOTES:

NOTES:

NOTES:

_____
_____
_____
_____
_____
_____
_____
_____
_____
_____
_____
_____
_____
_____
_____
_____
_____
_____
_____
_____
_____
_____
_____
_____
_____
_____
_____
_____
_____
_____
_____
_____